D1627202

FROM HOLIDAYS TO HOLY DAYS

FROM HOLIDAYS TO HOLY DAYS
A BENEDICTINE WALK THROUGH ADVENT

Albert Holtz, O.S.B.
Illustrations by the Author

MOREHOUSE PUBLISHING

Morehouse Publishing, 4775 Linglestown Road, Harrisburg, PA 17112

Morehouse Publishing, 445 Fifth Avenue, New York, NY 10016

Morehouse Publishing is an imprint of Church Publishing Incorporated.

Cover image: Herald Square and Macy's at night, NYC, by Bud Freund / courtesy of IndexOpen.com

Cover design by Brenda Klinger

Library of Congress Cataloging-in-Publication Data

Holtz, Albert.
  From holidays to holy days : a Benedictine walk through Advent / Albert Holtz.
      p. cm.
  Includes bibliographical references.
  ISBN 978-0-8192-2316-6 (pbk.)
  1. Advent—Meditations. 2. Christmas—Meditations. 3. Benedictines—Spiritual life. I. Title.
  BV40.H65 2008
  242'.332—dc22   2008024160

Printed in the United States of America

08 09 10 11 12 13   10 9 8 7 6 5 4 3 2 1

CONTENTS

INTRODUCTION

Holidays

Each year, just before Thanksgiving, the "holidays" begin: Santa Claus figures and candy canes appear in store windows, wreaths and Christmas trees begin to brighten bank lobbies, and milling crowds start filling shopping malls. For several weeks, into early January, the "holiday season" pervades almost every aspect of our lives: there are holiday songs on the radio and holiday movies and commercials on television, holiday postage stamps, and even holiday junk mail. We put up holiday decorations in our homes and expend immense amounts of time, effort, and money preparing for and celebrating the holidays—Christmas shopping accounts for a large percentage of the total annual sales of many retailers. The season progresses through office parties and holiday programs in schools, until last-minute shopping brings the pre-Christmas rush to a fever pitch. Then, with Christmas and New Year's Day, the holidays come to an abrupt end.

But, just at the moment that merchants and shoppers begin their hectic preparations for Christmas, the church begins a period of quiet reflection in joyful anticipation of that same event.

Advent

As far back as the fourth century, Christians have been observing Advent as a time of preparation for the coming of Christ at Christmas. In fact, Advent prepares for two different comings: the first is Jesus' birth at Bethlehem two thousand years ago, and the second is his final coming at the end of time. The various themes of Advent lead us back and forth between the two poles: the fact that God has already acted decisively on our behalf in Jesus' birth and the acknowledgement that there is still much work to be done to bring the kingdom to completion.

Advent starts out quietly, the mass readings and orations pointing out that the kingdom is, in fact, already present in our midst. Then, on the second Sunday of Advent, the pace picks up when John the Baptist enters the scene proclaiming his message of repentance. By the third week the season is building to a crescendo: beginning on December 17, the readings start to focus on the first coming of Christ in the flesh, including the gospel accounts of the annunciation, the visitation, and the birth of John the Baptist. Finally, the climax comes with the birth of Jesus at Christmas, a celebration that the church prolongs for a full week.

Holidays and Holy Days

The frantic activity of shopping and getting ready for the "holidays" provides a striking contrast to the quiet reflection and joyful, patient waiting that mark the "holy days" of Advent. Not surprisingly, the religious significance of Advent and Christmas tends to get lost amid all the shopping, housecleaning, decorating, and visiting that fill our holidays from the end of November through New Year's Day. How can we Christians hold on to the deeper spiritual meaning of our religious feasts during this busy time? One answer lies in the nature of Advent itself as a time for quiet reflection and contemplation.

My favorite definition of contemplation is "a long, loving look at the real." This description fits nicely into the theology of Saint Benedict of Nursia (ca. 480–ca. 546), whose *Rule for Monks* still provides the inspiration for the monastic life that we Benedictines follow. He bases his rule on two fundamental principles. The first is that God is present everywhere—he says that the monastery's tools should be treated with the same reverence as the sacred vessels of the altar. The second principle is that Christ is present in every single person we meet—most especially in the sick, the poor, and the pilgrim.

So, if we are trying to maintain a deep and meaningful spirituality of Advent and Christmas—while at the same time living in the hectic round of Christmas shopping and decorating—why not devote some of our Advent reflections to taking a long, loving look at the realities of the holiday season?

If Benedict is correct, we should be able to find in them some good spiritual insights into the mysteries of Advent and Christmas. This book is a series of just such meditations on the holiday realities that I have observed during my daily walks through the streets of Newark.

Walking around Newark

To follow my walks more meaningfully, the reader might profit from a few words of background information. I have been a Benedictine monk for almost fifty years and am a member of Newark Abbey. Like many Benedictine monasteries over the centuries, Newark Abbey is situated on a hill. Unlike most others, however, it is also located in the center of a city—the largest one in New Jersey. Three or four times a week, I step out of the front door of the monastery and go for a long walk around downtown Newark, getting exercise while observing the everyday life of the city and its people.

The downtown business and shopping district begins three blocks downhill and east of the monastery. After another seven blocks of stores and office buildings, past the train station, are the old immigrant neighborhoods of my favorite part of the city, the so-called Ironbound section (its name coming from the fact that for years it was surrounded by railroads on every side). Sometimes, however, instead of walking downtown, I'll walk north, along our own street, Dr. Martin Luther King Jr. Boulevard, to visit the three college campuses there.

The northeastern boundary of the city is the winding Passaic River, which brought the Englishman Robert Treat and the other founders from Connecticut Colony to this place in 1666. Sometimes, when I have an hour or more, I'll walk across the Bridge Street Bridge, through the town of Harrison, and return via the Jackson Street Bridge into the Ironbound section and back up the hill to the monastery.

The Book

This book is a series of brief meditations based on my walks around the city during the holiday season—or, better, during the holy days of Advent and Christmas—one for each day from the first Sunday of Advent through January 1. Each day's reflection is based on some familiar aspect of the holidays, such as Christmas shopping, welcoming guests, or putting up lights. The reader is invited to walk beside me and share in my reflections as I watch the city prepare for and then celebrate the holidays. Each chapter includes questions for reflection, a quotation from Sacred Scripture, and a passage from the *Rule of Benedict* or some other early monastic source.

I hope that these short but loving looks at the real will help you to discover in the familiar experiences of the holidays the deeper meaning of the holy days.

SUNDAY OF THE FIRST WEEK
Times and Seasons

This morning I celebrated mass for the first Sunday of Advent, marking the start of a new season in the church's calendar and the beginning of a new liturgical year. This afternoon I'm on my daily walk, heading down the hill from the monastery toward the downtown shopping district. From the window of the big Rite-Aid drugstore across the street, the Santa dolls and Christmas tree ornaments greet me like old friends—they've been there since the day after Halloween.

Storekeepers have a different calendar from the rest of us. They mark "seasons" by changing the merchandise displayed on their shelves: summer is replaced by back-to-school, which is replaced by Halloween, and Halloween by the Christmas holidays. Each year they seem to start the Christmas season a little earlier, hoping to squeeze in a few more shopping days.

As I cross Washington Street, the boxes of tinsel and the inflatable Santas that I see in the Rite-Aid window ahead start me thinking about the deeper implications of the idea of "season." When biblical writers wrote about a "season" they used the Greek word *kairos*, which is often translated "time," but they meant a time for some specific purpose—an occasion or an opportunity. It's the word used in the familiar passage in Ecclesiastes: " . . . and a time for every matter under heaven. A time to be born, and a time to die" (Eccles. 3:1–8). Paul writes to the Galatians, "So then, whenever we have an opportunity [*kairos*], let us work for the good of all" (Gal. 6:10). In fact, every moment of our lives is a *kairos*, a sacred "season," a chapter in the unfolding story of God's love for the world. For a Christian, life is made up of millions of unique moments, each one a *kairos*, an opportunity that will never come again. Every task we start, every decision we make, whether trivial or great, is a special time, a chance to build up the kingdom. Every encounter with another person is a unique *kairos*, a season for loving. Whether we're working, cooking supper, or relaxing in front of the television, each moment is a part of the story of God's loving presence in the world. It is all *kairos*.

"Time" or "season" in the Bible usually conveys a feeling of urgency, of an opportunity not to be missed. It is not surprising that the word comes up in various biblical readings during Advent. Paul uses it when he writes to the Corinthians: "Behold, now is the acceptable time, behold now is the day of salvation" (2 Cor. 6:2). In this morning's second reading at mass, Paul tells the Romans, "You know what time [*kairos*] it is, how it is now the moment for you to wake from sleep. For salvation is nearer to us now than when we became believers; the night is far gone, the day is near" (Rom. 13:11–12).

As I walk past the shops and glance into their windows full of Christmas decorations and gift boxes wrapped to look like presents, they all seem to be sending the same message: The "season" is upon us and we had better act right away. Interesting, I think, how the holiday "season" echoes Advent's biblical *kairos*; both of them carry an urgent message, a challenge that demands an immediate response. The time to act is not tomorrow. It was not yesterday. It is today, right now.

Since I'm great at procrastinating, the Advent readings sometimes unnerve me with their warnings that the hour is at hand or that now is the time to rise from sleep. This is especially true when it comes to spiritual things. I find handy excuses: "I have to finish this project first, then I'll do my spiritual reading." "Tomorrow I'll get more serious about praying." "Pretty soon I'll have to start to try to control my short temper."

As I continue to make my way past store windows filled with all sorts of holiday merchandise, I see the store owners' message clearly. A three-foot high Santa Claus figure in a store window seems to be calling out the biblical warning: "Albert, it's the season!" Then a Christmas tree decorated with blinking lights sparkles its message: "This is the season! Act now!" Everywhere I look on Market Street this afternoon, the idea is the same. This is not a time for delaying. Or, as Saint Paul would say, "Behold, now is the acceptable time, behold now is the day of salvation."

Reflection

Your life is made up of millions of unique moments, each one an opportunity that will never come again. How might you use Advent to make yourself more aware of these special opportunities in your own life? Is there some decision or task that you have been putting off but that you could address right now as a response to Advent's urgent call?

Sacred Scripture

"Take heed, watch; for you do not know when the time [*kairos*] will come." (Mark 13:33)

Rule of Benedict

Let us get up then, at long last, for the scriptures rouse us when they say: It is high time for us to arise from sleep. (Prologue, v. 8)

MONDAY OF THE FIRST WEEK
Holiday Music

I'm strolling along a crowded sidewalk on Broad Street across from the new Prudential Center sports arena. An amplifier is pouring loud rap music onto the crowd passing the electronics store. Even though it's only the first week of Advent, I would really prefer some Christmas music. Of course, several radio stations have already started playing their traditional mixture of songs about snowflakes and mistletoe interspersed with traditional religious carols and hymns. When the two kinds of Christmas music are mixed together like that, I've noticed that the non-religious songs—about chestnuts roasting and partridges in pear trees—start to resonate somehow with the sacred songs and begin to echo the deep religious themes of Advent and Christmas. "Santa Claus Is Coming to Town" starts to reflect the joyful longing that underlies "O Come, O Come, Emmanuel." Sentimental songs like "I'll be Home for Christmas" start to pick up the sincere warmth and love of "It Came Upon a Midnight Clear." The lyrics of "Silver Bells" begin to blend with the message of heartfelt peace and gladness of "Joy to the World."

As I continue down the noisy sidewalk thinking about Christmas songs, it occurs to me that the act of singing itself is such a deeply moving human experience that many cultures consider it something sacred and mystical. I remember reading a creation myth that told of how the world was actually sung into existence. Then I start to picture the scene in heaven at the first moment of creation. Surely, I think to myself, God's words of creation could not have been simply spoken like so many simple instructions; no, they must have been sung to an exquisitely beautiful melody. "Let there be light" was no spoken command but rather the first line of a spontaneous love song that is still overflowing from the Creator's heart.

As I keep walking, the sun is reflecting from the windows of some buildings on the other side of Broad Street. I start to imagine the sun and the planets in their silent march across the heavens, still echoing the divine song of creation, as do the birds and other animals with their songs and cries. All our human music, too, is simply an echo of that first music that still resounds in our hearts: a raga from India, an Andean song played on a charango, a complicated piece on a Senegalese kora harp. Each of these is an echo of God's own voice on the first day of creation. So when we hear a holiday song that is not about Jesus but about a winter wonderland, we can still hear in it the harmonies of heaven, traces of the Lord's own voice celebrating joy, contentment, and longing, the very themes the church echoes in her liturgy during Advent and Christmas.

I'm at the corner of Branford Place, threading my way through a small crowd of teenagers gathered around a pushcart, sorting through CD's of rap, hip-hop, and reggae. A young man is presiding watchfully over the scene as a reggae tune blasts from the boom box he has chained to his cart. It's not at all what you could call "Christmas" music or "sacred music." But as I turn left up Branford place toward the monastery, I think I can hear in its exuberance a faint echo of the first melody ever sung, the one that goes "Let there be light!"

On my way up the hill I start to hum a beautiful Gregorian chant tune, the song for vespers in Advent: *Conditor Alme Siderum* ("Dear Maker of the Starry Skies").

Reflection

Take a favorite Advent hymn and meditate on its words. Here are two verses of a modern carol first published in *The Oxford Book of Carols* in 1928:

People, look east. The time is near
Of the crowning of the year.
Make your house fair as you are able,
Trim the hearth and set the table.
People, look east and sing today:
Love, the Guest is on the way.

Angels announce with shouts of mirth,
Him who brings new life to earth.

Set every peak and valley humming
With the word, the Lord is coming
People, look east and sing today:
Love, the Lord, is on the way.[1]

—Eleanor Farjeon

Sacred Scripture

Praise for God's Surpassing Greatness

Praise him with trumpet sound;
praise him with lute and harp!
Praise him with tambourine and dance;
praise him with strings and pipe!
Praise him with clanging cymbals;
praise him with loud clashing cymbals!
Let everything that breathes praise the Lord!
Praise the Lord! (Ps. 150:3–6)

Rule of Benedict

We must always remember, therefore, what the Prophet says: "Serve the Lord with fear," and again, "Sing praise wisely"; and, "In the presence of the angels I will sing to you." Let us consider, then, how we ought to behave in the presence of God and his angels, and let us stand to sing the psalms in such a way that our minds are in harmony with our voices. (Chapter 19, "The Discipline of Psalmody," vv. 3–7)

---

1. "People Look East," in Percy Dearmer, R. Vaughan Williams, and Martin Shaw, *The Oxford Book of Carols* (Oxford: Oxford University Press, 1985). Used with permission of David Higham Associates, LTD.

TUESDAY OF THE FIRST WEEK
Salvation Army

U p ahead, just outside the main entrance to Newark's Penn Station, stands a man in a heavy winter coat and a dark blue cap. Beside him, hanging on a tripod, is a red bucket labeled "Salvation Army."

I slow down so I can watch this interesting fellow with his pleasant, peaceful expression set off by rimless glasses. Although the commuters rushing past don't seem to notice him, he appears quite content to just stay right where he is, as if he knows that he's doing something worthwhile. He stamps his feet a couple of times on the cold sidewalk and gives his hand-bell another shake.

Watching him I start to think about how the holidays bring out people's generosity: the Children's Christmas Fund, Toys for Tots, food drives, and other charitable collections have been a traditional part of the holiday season for centuries.

For Christians, however, bringing comfort to the poor and afflicted is not just a seasonal whim but is at the very center of Jesus' message. Again and again the gospels show him being moved with compassion. The story of the miracle of the loaves and fishes, for instance, begins, "At the sight of the crowds, [Jesus'] heart was moved with pity for them" (Matt. 9:36), and the raising of the widow's son starts with Jesus' being "moved with pity" (Luke 7:13). During this first week of Advent, the church reflects on various signs that the kingdom is already present among us; surely one of the most powerful of these is people's generosity toward their less fortunate brothers and sisters.

Now I'm curious: will someone actually come by and put in a contribution? Just then, a woman in a threadbare coat and an inexpensive knit hat slows down to put something in the red bucket, smiling at the man as he gives her a cheerful thank you. The generosity of this woman reminds me that Jesus' point is not simply that I should feel compassion for others. The holidays fill many of us with warm and generous feelings of "good will toward all." Of itself, however, compassion is not a sign of the kingdom; it is not even a virtue—it is just an emotion. Nowhere does Jesus say that on judgment day God is going to ask me how I felt about anyone. Nor does he promise that the divine Judge will congratulate me with the words, "When I was hungry, you felt bad for me; when I was thirsty you felt sad for me, when I was in prison you felt awful about it." No, just as compassion moves Jesus to take action—to heal, or forgive, or feed, even to restore to life—it has to move me to compassionate action like this woman's.

Her simple generosity reminds me that I will become Christlike then, not by feeling compassion for a needy neighbor or for someone sick in the hospital, but rather by doing something to help. Saint Benedict reflects this idea in several places in his *Rule for Monks*. For example, he warns that "[the monastery cellarer] must show every care and concern for the sick, children, guests and the poor, knowing for certain that he will be held accountable for all of them on the day of judgment" (RB 31:9). He calls for actions, not just feelings.

A middle-aged man in a dark overcoat and a white scarf pauses at the Salvation Army bucket. Reaching into his pocket he pulls out a small wad of bills, peels off a couple and drops them in. Another pleasant "Thank you!" from the man in the blue coat as he rings his handbell a couple of times.

These generous people are good reminders for me to move beyond the mere warm, charitable feelings of "the Christmas spirit" to real works of charity. During Advent we wait and pray for the coming of the kingdom, but the kingdom becomes present on earth not because of the way people feel but because of the way they act. If I want to help bring that kingdom to its completion, I will have to go out of my way, forgetting my own comfort and convenience to visit a sick friend, postponing my own plans to take some extra time with a student, and ignoring my preoccupations to give encouragement to someone who needs it.

Just then, another woman comes by and tosses something in. The man with the rimless glasses smiles his thanks. I realize that I'm getting cold standing here on the sidewalk, so I turn from the man and his red bucket and continue on my way, encouraged and challenged by the generosity of three people who have just helped make the kingdom a little more present in Penn Station Newark. From behind me, the sound of the Salvation Army handbell seems to follow me on the cold wind.

Reflection

As we await during Advent God's ultimate act of compassion, the coming of our Savior, we have plenty of opportunities to be compassionate to others. Think of one or two steps you might take to put compassion into action during Advent. You may want to ask God to point out to you someone who especially needs your help during this holy season.

Sacred Scripture

"Now by chance a priest was going down that road; and when he saw him, he passed by on the other side. So likewise a Levite, when he came to the place and saw him, passed by on the other side. But a Samaritan while traveling came near him; and when he saw him, he was moved with pity. He went to him and bandaged his wounds, having poured oil and wine on them. Then he put him on his own animal, brought him to an inn, and took care of him." (Luke 10:31–34)

Rule of Benedict

You must relieve the lot of the poor, clothe the naked, visit the sick, and bury the dead. Go to help the troubled and console the sorrowing. (Chapter 4, "The Instruments for Good Works," vv. 14–19)

WEDNESDAY OF THE
FIRST WEEK
Christmas Wreaths

The clear night sky is strewn with bright pinpoints of cold light that stand against the blackness of space as I make my way back to the monastery from the school's residence hall. I've just spent an hour helping a couple of students prepare for a test and then stayed to pray Night Prayer with the sixty-some boarders. Now I'm heading for the pedestrian bridge that will take me through the school to the monastery on the other side of King Boulevard.

Despite the biting cold I stop to look up at the wide expanse of stars—a rare sight for us city-dwellers—and easily pick out Orion, the dippers, and Cassiopeia. I look back at the handsome brick façade of the residence hall and over its entrance the large Christmas wreath sparkling with dozens of tiny electric bulbs.

I turn and continue on my homeward route, which will take me through the gymnasium. As I get to the gym, I notice on its door another wreath, a small evergreen one with a red ribbon. The gym, it occurs to me, is the perfect place for a

Christmas wreath. In ancient Greece, wreaths made of laurel leaves were awarded to winning athletes in the Olympic Games. Maybe it was some victorious Olympic athlete who first hung his wreath on a wall as a souvenir of his prowess, but in any case, for thousands of years now, in many places around the world, different kinds of wreaths have been decorating walls, doors, and windows.

Before going through the door I step over to the railing at the edge of the little terrace that looks down onto the sidewalk and street one story below. Directly across from me are the monastery and the school buildings. When I notice the wreaths on the abbey's front door and over the entrance to the church, I remember that the athlete's wreath became an important image for the earliest Christians.[2] Paul tells the Corinthians, "Athletes exercise self-control in all things; they do it to receive a perishable garland [wreath, crown], but we an imperishable one" (1 Cor. 9:25), Peter writes, "And when the chief shepherd appears, you will win the crown of glory that never fades away" (1 Pet. 5:4), and the Book of Revelation promises, "Be faithful until death, and I will give you the crown of life" (Rev. 2:10).

Taking on our flesh at Christmas, Christ became one of us in order to conquer sin and death. Maybe that's why Christians started hanging wreaths at Christmas—as signs of Jesus' victory. But there's more to the story of wreaths. In a beautiful and familiar passage, Saint Paul assures us that there is a victor's wreath waiting for each of us as well: "I have fought the good fight, I have finished the race, I have kept the faith. From now on there is reserved for me the crown [wreath, garland] of righteousness, which the Lord, the righteous judge, will give to me on that day, and not only to me but also to all who have longed for his appearing" (2 Tim. 4:7–8).

Christmas wreaths, then, are double reminders: they recall our Savior's victory over death, and they challenge me to lead my earthly life in a way worthy of the heavenly crown that has been laid up for me. It is this second meaning that is the troublesome one. A wreath is a reward for victory, and so it asks me a pointed question: what victories have you won recently? Have you overcome your impatience with that certain person? Have you overcome your offhand attitude at prayer? Are you truly keeping your eyes on the prize that doesn't wither away as earthly rewards do?

Beginning to feel the cold, I finally turn toward the door of the gym. There, staring at me with a wordless challenge, is the Christmas wreath.

---

2. The Greek noun *stephanos* means both "wreath" and "crown," depending on the context.

Reflection

Christmas wreaths can serve to remind you to lead a life worthy of the "crown of life" that has been laid up for you in heaven. Think of some practice you might undertake during Advent, or one you are already doing: perhaps some extra prayer each day, or an effort to be especially kind to someone you find difficult to get along with. Then every time you see a Christmas wreath let it remind you of your Advent resolution and of the victor's wreath in heaven that has your name on it.

Sacred Scripture

Blessed is anyone who endures temptation. Such a one has stood the test and will receive the crown of life that the Lord has promised to those who love him. (James 1:12)

Rule of Benedict

The second step of humility is that a man loves not his own will nor takes pleasure from the satisfaction of his desires; rather he shall imitate by his actions that saying of the Lord: "I have come not to do my own will, but the will of him who sent me." Similarly we read, "Consent merits punishment; constraint wins a crown." (Chapter 7, "On Humility," vv. 31–38)

THURSDAY OF THE FIRST WEEK
Preparing

The imposing Greek façade of the Newark Museum looks the same as it always does: solemn, stately, and gray. Farther down Washington Street, next door to the museum, is a three-story red brick and limestone mansion, the Ballantine House. Built in 1885 for the beer baron John H. Ballantine, it is a proud reminder of the days when Newark was one of the richest industrial centers in America. Now a National Historic Landmark, it is part of the Newark Museum. I remember visiting it once and enjoying the holiday display in the dining room that featured a table set for an elaborate late Victorian Christmas dinner with the Ballantines. There were evergreen garlands and holly, and red ribbons dropping from the chandelier to the table, each with a little wrapped present attached to the end. Silverware and crystal sparkled on the dazzling white tablecloth around a monumental Christmas pudding.

As my empty stomach rumbles at the thought of the pudding, I keep walking, passing in front of the Ballantine House, musing on the hectic preparations that must have gone on there before such a banquet. The servants of the wealthy family must have worked extra hard in the weeks before the Christmas and New Years' Eve celebrations to make sure everything would be exactly right.

For most of us, much of the holiday season is spent getting ready: decorating the house, buying presents, planning family get-togethers, and arranging dates to visit friends. Far from being a distraction from our keeping of Advent, however, these preparations can remind us that Advent is meant precisely to be a time for preparing for the coming of Christ at Christmas. On the Second Sunday of Advent each year the church has us listen to John the Baptist, the great forerunner of Jesus, crying out, "Prepare the way of the Lord, make his paths straight" (Mark 1:3). Isaiah tells us of "the voice of him that crieth in the wilderness, Prepare ye the way of the Lord, make straight in the desert a highway for our God. Every valley shall be exalted, and every mountain and hill shall be made low: and the crooked shall be made straight, and the rough places plain" (Isa. 40:3–4 KJV).

This kind of inward preparing, however, requires a good knowledge of the local terrain: we have to be acquainted with the valleys in our lives—the sinful habits, say, or the oppressive memories that weigh us down. We have to know the mountains in our hearts, too—the hills of vanity, the peaks of presumption and pride. We need to recognize the twists that our stubbornness has put in our life's road. With a little introspection we'll find that there is plenty of preparing to be done in our hearts while we're doing our other holiday preparations. Getting our homes ready for Christmas becomes an outward sign of the true but invisible work of Advent: preparing our hearts.

I stop in front of the old mansion, and I notice that it looks somber and a bit forlorn, full of ghosts of Christmases past. The golden era of elegant holiday parties that once enlivened the house is long gone: no more bustling preparations, no last-minute rush to make sure everything is just so.

Then, as I continue past the mansion, I glance to my left down the side of the old house and realize just how big it is. There must be dozens of rooms, not counting the servants' quarters up in the attic—and all those guest rooms to be prepared for the holiday visitors. The guest rooms remind me of Jesus' promise to his disciples: "In my Father's house are many rooms; if it were not so, would I have told you that I go to prepare a place for you? And when I go and prepare a place for you, I will come again and will take you to myself, that where I am you may be also" (John 14:2, 3). In fact, most of the preparing that is spoken of in the Bible is being done by God, whether preparing a land for the Chosen People or a heavenly banquet on Mount Zion. All our holiday preparations—the shopping, the housecleaning and decorating, the cooking and card-writing—besides reminding us to prepare our hearts, serve as pale reflections of the preparations that God is making to welcome us one day into the kingdom that is being announced during Advent.

With the Ballantine House behind me, I keep thinking about all the preparations that Jesus is making right now, getting all those rooms ready in heaven—including, I trust, one for me.

Reflection

Ask Jesus to help you this Advent to prepare his way. Think of a couple of rough places in your life that need to be smoothed out to allow the Lord easier entry into your life. What about some heights that need to be lowered or a certain valley that needs to be filled in? Is one of these a project that might need to be worked on all year long?

Sacred Scripture

Then the King will say to those at his right hand, "Come, O blessed of my Father, inherit the kingdom prepared for you from the foundation of the world." (Matt. 25:34)

Rule of Benedict

If we wish to dwell in the tent of this kingdom, we will never arrive unless we run there by doing good deeds. But let us ask the Lord with the Prophet: Who will dwell in your tent, Lord; who will find rest upon your holy mountain? After this question, brothers, let us listen well to what the Lord says in reply, for he shows us the way to his tent. (Prologue, vv. 22–24)

FRIDAY OF THE FIRST WEEK
Memories

L ooming ahead as I walk through gusts of swirling snow is the gray, ten-story box that used to be Bamberger's department store. Now it is home to a large drugstore and number of small street-level shops. The upper floors are leased, I'm told, to some sort of Internet computer company.

As I cross Washington Street toward the old building, my mind takes me back over fifty years to when my parents would bring the whole family to Bamberger's to see Santa Claus. Each of the great store windows would offer a different holiday display: a winter snow scene, a Christmas tale, a collection of rare dolls or electric trains. Passing through the revolving doors, we would enter the intoxicating atmosphere of the scent of pine boughs and perfumes and pass through crowds of shoppers milling in the wide aisles as we made our way to the bank of elevators that would whisk us to the sixth-floor toy department—and to Santa.

I reach the curb in front of the drugstore, noticing the tire tracks left in the coating of new snow. It strikes me that so much of the magic of the holidays is based on our childhood memories: the aroma of Christmas cookies baking, the sound of familiar carols, the simple rituals of the Advent wreath or tree-trimming or the excited tearing of the wrapping paper off of a mysterious box. For many of us, these memories are the real heart of the Christmas holiday season.

Just as memories are a crucial part of the holiday experience, they are essential to our life as Christians as well. During Advent, for example, the church remembers the messianic predictions of the prophets: "Therefore the Lord himself will give you a sign. Look, the young woman is with child and shall bear a son, and shall name him Immanuel" (Isa. 7:14). "But you, O Bethlehem of Ephrathah, who are one of the little clans of Judah, from you shall come forth for me one who is to rule in Israel, whose origin is from of old, from ancient days" (Mic. 5:2).

With the drugstore behind me, and pushing against the wind and snow, I start passing the row of large plate-glass windows. I pause in front of one of them, imagining that it contains one of those magical Christmas scenes—Santa flying over snowy, moonlit rooftops in his sleigh, with tiny stars sparkling in the dark sky. Suddenly I'm brought back by my reflection in the window—not that of a little boy but of a man in his sixties. The window actually contains stacks of neatly folded stone-washed jeans and turtleneck sweaters. I keep walking.

Remembering is at the heart not only of Advent but of the Christmas season as we retell and meditate on the marvelous story of Christmas. We recall Gabriel's visit to Mary, the birth in a stable at Bethlehem, the visit by shepherds who have just seen a multitude of the heavenly host and have now come to see the baby wrapped in swaddling clothes. Then there are the exotic wise men with their camels and their gifts.

Retelling the stories also helped the early Christians to gain perspective on their own lives. Recalling how Jesus suffered persecution helped them to endure the persecution they themselves were suffering. Remembering how he cured paralytics, drove out demons, and calmed storms gave them courage to call on him for help in their own need.

And today our own remembering of the prophecies and of the words and deeds of Jesus helps us make sense of our own experiences as well: each person's life is a story, a part of the one beautiful love story recounted in the Bible. When I am facing some important or unsettling experience or trying to deal with some awful tragedy, it helps if I can remember that I am part of the ongoing story of God's faithful love, and, even if I can't understand it at the time, I can believe that my whole life makes sense because it belongs to that larger story.

Now, as I continue walking with the crowd of shoppers, I find myself at the corner of Halsey Street and turn left into a steady wind to finish my tour of Bamberger's windows. The front of a shoe store takes up what used to be two windows, then comes a clothing boutique, while a fourth space that once glowed with warm Christmas images is dark and empty, protected by a roll-down security grill. There are no more of those magical Christmas windows.

When I notice the snow starting to form a white carpet on the pavement, a flood of childhood memories wells up. I can hear my own shouts of delight as the toboggan picks up speed and careens down the hill, the icy wind whistling past my ears. Suddenly I'm startled to find myself already at the corner of Bank Street. Smiling at the memories of toboggans and magical store windows, I say a little prayer of thanks to God for giving me the gift of memories and for letting me know that I am part of the one great story—the Lord's ageless love affair with creation.

Reflection

Your life is an integral part of the wider story of God's infinite, ongoing love for the world. Think of some personal memories that you associate with Christmas time, and ask yourself how these fit into the story of your relationship with God. Try using the ancient Christian practice of putting things into perspective by seeing them as reflecting the experience of someone in the Bible: if some of your memories are unhappy or unpleasant, you can identify with the fear that the Israelites felt as God led them out into the wilderness; if you're confused, reflect on the perplexity that the Virgin Mary must have felt when hearing Gabriel's' message in Nazareth. On a good day you may want to sing with Miriam as she shouts her song of victory after Israel has escaped through the Red Sea.

Sacred Scripture

Long ago God spoke to our ancestors in many and various ways by the prophets, but in these last days he has spoken to us by a Son, whom he appointed heir of all things, through whom he also created the worlds. He is the reflection of God's glory and the exact imprint of God's very being, and he sustains all things by his powerful word. (Heb. 1:1–3)

Wisdom of Saint Athanasius

And it seems to me that [the words of the psalms] become like a mirror to the person singing them, that he might perceive himself and the emotions of his soul, and thus affected, he might recite them. For in fact he who hears the one reading receives the song that is recited as being about him, and either, when he is convicted

by his conscience, being pierced, he will repent, or hearing of the
hope that resides in God, and of the succor available to believers . . .
he exults and begins to give thanks to God. (*Letter to Marcellinus*)[3]

---

3. Robert C. Gregg, trans. and intro., *Athanasius: The Life of Antony and the Letter
    to Marcellinus* (Mahwah, NJ: Paulist Press, 1980), 111.

Saturday of the First Week
"What Do You Want for Christmas?"

I am walking north on Broad Street, slowed by the crowds of shoppers, when I notice two children on the sidewalk standing very still, staring through the plate glass window of the toy store. The boy is about eleven or twelve years old. Standing beside him, in a puffy pink coat with the hood up, is a little girl who barely reaches his elbow. He is holding her hand protectively, the way big brothers do. Their noses are almost touching the plate

glass of the toy store's window, which is crammed for Christmas with dozens of bright-colored toys, dolls, and electronic games. I can't see their faces, but their rapt, transfixed pose stirs up my own memory of a powerful emotion: wanting a certain something for Christmas and wishing for it so hard I would start to ache inside.

I keep moving on past the two children who have not stirred and start to think how they make a good image of the basic human need that underlies Advent: all of us, whether we know it or not, are longing and hoping for something to fill our emptiness. Wanting is simply part of being human— it comes with not being God, being incomplete. We're always searching relentlessly, sometimes even desperately, to fill the void inside of us.

St. Augustine thinks that all our human hungers and all our yearnings are simply facets of one single, inborn longing: the desire for the Divine. My fondness for chocolate ice cream, my attraction to a pretty face, and my passion for Mozart's horn concertos are all aspects of the one deepest desire, to possess God. In Augustine's view, we are each born with a natural thirst for the Divine, which only something Infinite can ultimately satisfy. Advertisers know about this inner longing; they redirect it, converting it into a desire for a flashy car, the latest video game, or this year's "must-have" toy. Millions of us fall for this switch because we don't understand the real goal of our inner hunger. Under the spell of advertisers, political demagogues, and others, we get caught up in a frenzied, frantic seeking after created things such as material possessions, power, or comfort.

Ironically, this misguided passionate searching is most apparent during the pre-Christmas shopping frenzy, which occurs during Advent, the very season when the church keeps pointing us toward the true object of our longing: the only one who can fill the nagging emptiness at the center of our hearts. The message of Advent has never been more needed than it is in our day, when so many people are caught up in a frantic but misdirected search for happiness.

As I head toward the next corner, I start noticing the faces of the people coming toward me. Some seem preoccupied or distracted, others look rushed, and a few even seem angry. But maybe, I think, these are all the different faces of the same sense of incompleteness, of longing for something more. Ultimately, Augustine would say, they are all longing for God.

I stop at the corner across from Starbucks to wait for the light to change. A young teenager standing beside me, wearing tiny earphones, is clutching a small plastic bag from the electronics store in the middle of the block. I try to guess what's in his bag: A new video game? An MP3 player? The light changes, and my attention is drawn toward the wave of people charging toward us in the crosswalk, many of them carrying shopping bags as well.

In his *Rule for Monks*, St. Benedict demands that any new aspirants to the community "truly seek God." He orders the entire life of the monastery toward this seeking: poverty and silence, stability and holy reading, caring for the sick and waiting tables; everything is carefully designed to keep us focused on our single-minded search for God.

But Benedict, a wise student of human nature, also knows that his monks will get distracted from time to time, whether by unruly appetites, by anger and other emotions, or by discouragement. I've certainly forgotten the one true goal myself from time to time, and have gone instead after pursuits contrary to or at least different from the only one that matters. Sometimes I have aimed at my own comfort or convenience, at other times I have tried to accomplish my own agenda instead of God's. But sooner or later grace has always called me back each time, reminding me what I am really striving for and longing for: the one thing necessary.

I get to the other curb and continue along Broad Street with the shoppers, all of us seeking and hoping, searching and striving. I say a little prayer that during Advent, the season of hope, we can all realize that we all have only one real and final fulfillment, Jesus Christ, for whose coming we watch and pray. "O Come, Divine Messiah!"

Reflection

Saint Augustine wrote that all of our longings and desires are actually part of the one single desire for the Infinite. Think of some passionate longings of yours, such as your love for a specific person, or a certain goal you are striving for. Reflect on each of these, asking yourself how this longing helps you in your quest to get closer to God. Is your longing for God as intense and passionate as this particular desire?

Sacred Scripture

"As a deer longs for flowing streams,
so my soul longs for you, O God.
My soul thirsts for God,
for the living God.
When shall I come and behold
the face of God?" (Ps. 42:1–2)

Wisdom of Saint Basil

Men are by nature, then, desirous of the beautiful. But, that which is truly beautiful and desirable is the good. Now, the good is God, and, since all creatures desire good, therefore all creatures desire God. (*The Long Rules*, Q.2)[4]

---

4. Saint Basil, *The Long Rules-I* (Boston: St. Paul Editions, 1950), 21.

SUNDAY OF THE SECOND WEEK
Street Decorations

I'm driving home after saying Sunday morning mass in a nearby parish. As I turn onto South Orange Avenue and start down the half-mile hill toward the center of downtown, I smile to myself. Stretching ahead of me, holiday banners on the lampposts lining both sides of the street form a colorful corridor of candles, snowmen, and giant snowflakes. When I was a youngster, the Christmas decorations on South Orange Avenue would reach across the roadway on wires to form a welcoming pathway of lights and garlands, like a festive outdoor tunnel leading everyone toward Christmas.

I think of that tunnel as I drive between two rows of banners leading all the way down the hill; it occurs to me that they are ideal for getting Christians ready for Christmas. The practice of decorating streets for special occasions, which goes back to a custom in the Greek world before the time of Christ, is one of the most direct reminders of the real meaning of Advent. In the ancient days, when some high-ranking person, especially a king or an emperor, was coming to visit a province, the roads along the route would be decorated in honor of the visiting dignitary, and the citizens would come out of the city to escort the honored visitor through their gates. Such an official visit was called a *parousia* in Greek. For example, one ancient text speaks of a province "looking forward to the coming [*parousia*] of Antiochus."

In the New Testament, the word *parousia* came to refer to what was to become one of the most important themes of the Advent season, the second coming of Christ as King at the end of time. In the gospel of Matthew, the disciples ask Jesus, "Tell us, when will this be, and what will be the sign of your coming and of the close of the age?" (Matt. 24:3). He replies, "For as the lightning comes from the east and shines as far as the west, so will be the coming of the Son of man" (Matt. 24:27).

As I continue down the banner-lined avenue toward the buildings of downtown, I wonder if Jesus will make his triumphal way down a street like this at his final coming. If he does, how will I feel as I stand there along the curb? Will I be happy, or worried, or wishing I had more time to get ready? I start to feel uneasy as I picture myself standing there embarrassed at being caught by surprise, with lots of unfinished business that will now remain forever undone: an apology that will never be given, a prayer that will never be said, a thank you that will never be spoken.

The parousia will be bad news only for people who have rejected God's rule over their lives, which is why Saint Benedict warns in the Holy Rule: "Live in fear of judgment day" (RB 4:44; 7:64). But during Advent the church celebrates the fact that for those who are prepared, the parousia is a time of glory and reward, of resurrection and blessing, something to look forward to. James writes in his epistle, "Therefore be patient, brethren, until the coming of the Lord. See how the farmer waits for the precious fruit of the earth, waiting patiently for it until it receives the early and latter rain. You also be patient. Establish your hearts, for the coming of the Lord is at hand" (James 5:7–8 NKJV). For them, the second coming would be a joyous royal visit and a time of blessing. Paul writes to the Christians at Thessalonica, "Now may the God of peace Himself sanctify you completely; and may your whole spirit, soul, and body be preserved blameless at the [parousia] of our Lord Jesus Christ" (1 Thess. 5:23 NKJV).

As I continue driving down the corridor of festive banners, I again start to imagine him entering Newark along this long parade route: the curbs of South Orange Avenue will be lined with crowds shouting and clapping, waving and welcoming the Lord into our city as he comes not just on a royal visit but to deliver us all at last from the grip of sin, suffering, and death.

As I near the bottom of the hill, my monastery and our school buildings come into view. In the distance, the buildings of Newark's skyline stand against a great bank of white clouds that glow in the midmorning sunlight. Jesus' words come to mind right away: "You will see the Son of man seated at the right hand of Power, and coming on the clouds of heaven" (Matt. 26:64). Maybe he'll come on some mighty clouds like those just above the Prudential building.

But as I drive past the last banner, I change my mind. I think the Lord will certainly come right down South Orange Avenue, welcomed by cheering crowds along a colorful corridor of banners of candles, snowmen, and giant snowflakes.

Reflection

Saint Benedict says that a monk ought always to keep death before his eyes, that is, to behave as he would if he knew that Christ were about to arrive. It is difficult to maintain that kind of awareness, but you might take the opportunity right now to ask yourself if there is some behavior you need to change, or some unfinished business that you have been postponing. Let the holiday decorations you see along the street remind you that one day Christ will indeed return in glory—you just don't know when.

Sacred Scripture

Now may our God and Father himself and our Lord Jesus direct our way to you. And may the Lord make you increase and abound in love for one another and for all, just as we abound in love for you. And may he so strengthen your hearts in holiness that you may be blameless before our God and Father at the coming of our Lord Jesus with all his saints. (1 Thess. 3:11–13)

Rule of Benedict

These, then, are the tools of the spiritual craft. When we have used them without ceasing day and night and have returned them on judgment day, our wages will be the reward the Lord has promised: "What the eye has not seen nor the ear heard, God has prepared for those who love him." (Chapter 4, "The Tools for Good Works," vv. 75–77)

Monday of the Second Week
Traffic Jam

I'm in my car on Route 21 in Newark, drumming my hands on the steering wheel, caught in the clutches of holiday gridlock. The truck in front of me crawls forward a few feet, so I ease my foot off the brake and inch up behind him. Even with the windows closed, the ominous smell of auto exhaust poisons the air—and my mood.

Not far ahead, where traffic from a bridge over the Passaic River crosses Route 21, angry drivers are beeping their horns in frustration. The tension is mounting. I now notice that I've been squeezing the steering wheel so hard that my fingers are starting to ache. I glance at my watch and see that I have less than half an hour to get to our five o'clock community mass in the monastery, where I am scheduled to give the homily. But here I sit, caught in a snarl of cars and trucks, helpless to change the situation. The fact that I could walk to the monastery from here in twenty minutes only makes my situation more exasperating. I can feel myself growing even more impatient. Hoping to avoid some of the exhaust fumes, I decide to leave a few feet of breathing room between me and the truck in front.

Suddenly, without any warning, a driver in the lane to my right turns sharply and starts to squeeze his car into my breathing space. I lean on my horn in a rage and step on the gas to keep him from cutting in front of me. "Idiot!" I shout as he steers his car back into the lane where it belongs.

Then, to make matters worse, I remember that I don't even have a homily prepared for mass yet. I start to think about a topic. I had recently preached about what Father Adrian Van Kaam calls the "gentle" approach to life's situations"[5]: we admit that we cannot control the undesirable situation, and, accepting it as a given, simply make the best of it. In my sermon I used his example of being stuck driving behind a slow-moving hay wagon on some back road; Father Van Kaam suggests that instead of railing and fuming or trying to pass illegally, we can choose to take advantage of the delay to appreciate the wildflowers along the roadside that we would never have noticed before.

When the truck crawls a few feet closer to the intersection, I deliberately tailgate, careful not to leave more than a foot between bumpers. The truck is not exactly a hay wagon, and there are few if any wildflowers to enjoy along the side of Route 21, but I decide to take Father Van Kaam's advice and just relax and accept the situation.

Maybe there's a homily here, I decide. I start to ask myself: Okay, what does getting caught in traffic have to do with Advent anyway? Or, better: What does the gentle approach to life have to do with Advent?

On the First Sunday of Advent, the Lord promised Israel, "Now, I will make of you a threshing-sledge, sharp, new, and having teeth; you shall thresh the mountains and crush them, and you shall make the hills like chaff" (Isa. 41:15). And John the Baptist called for leveling mountains and filling in valleys that were in the way, and laying the axe to the root of the tree. This is not exactly gentle talk!

Now the driver on my right, whom I fended off a moment ago, has pulled into the right-hand emergency stopping lane and is squeezing his car along the curb, barely missing dozens of door handles and side mirrors as he pushes ahead. I decide to ignore him and worry instead about my homily. If John the Baptist isn't much of a model of the gentle approach, it occurs to me that there is another central figure in Advent who is—the Virgin Mary.

She is a model of gentle acceptance, courageously choosing to do whatever the Lord's will is for her, telling the angel, "Here am I, the servant of the Lord; let it be with me according to your word" (Luke 1:38).

What about my own approach to life? How often do I try to force my will, my schedule, or my preconceived ideas onto the people and circumstances around me?

---

5. Adrian van Kaam, *Spirituality and the Gentle Life* (Denville, NJ: Dimension Books, 1974).

The honking of horns gets louder and more frequent. It's hot in the car, so I reach over and slide the heater control to off as I inch up to the traffic light at last. The truck ahead of me has just crept across the intersection on the amber light, leaving me at the red to watch the empty space in front of me fill up with cross-traffic. The driver who was sneaking up in the parking lane is now bullying his way through the middle of the intersection using his car like a threshing sledge, cutting a swath across the stream of cars coming from the bridge.

Suddenly I feel sorry for him, imagining what it must be like to go through life as a threshing sledge. Then I wince as I ask myself how often I look like a threshing sledge to the people around me. I say a little prayer asking that I may be able to share a little of the courageous Mary's gentle acceptance of life—even in such a mundane situation as this traffic jam.

Now, as I wait for the light to change to green, I notice that my grip on the steering wheel has relaxed. I check the clock on the dashboard. Only fifteen minutes to get to mass—but now I have my homily!

Reflection

In what situations or with what people are you most able to take a "gentle" approach and accept a situation you cannot change? When are you least likely to take that approach? Think of some stressful situation that is likely to come up during the holidays. How might you handle it with a "gentle" approach?

Sacred Scripture

[Paul and Timothy] traveled through the Phrygian and Galatian territory because they had been prevented by the Holy Spirit from preaching the message in the province of Asia. When they came to Mysia, they tried to go on into Bithynia, but the Spirit of Jesus did not allow them, so they crossed through Mysia and came down to Troas. During (the) night Paul had a vision. A Macedonian stood before him and implored him with these words, "Come over to Macedonia and help us." When he had seen the vision, we sought passage to Macedonia at once, concluding that God had called us to proclaim the good news to them. (Acts 16:6–10 NAB)

Wisdom of the Desert

Some monks came to see Abba Poemen and said to him, "When we see brothers dozing during the services in church, should we rouse them so that they can be watchful?" He said to them "For my part, when I see a brother dozing, I put his head on my knees and let him rest."[6]

---

6. Benedicta Ward, ed., *Daily Readings with the Fathers* (Springfield, IL: Templegate Publishers, 1990), 45.

TUESDAY OF THE SECOND WEEK
Wrapping Paper

I'm standing in front of a display of dozens of kinds of Christmas wrapping paper, daunted by too many colors and designs and by having to choose one of them. Although I have only a couple of small presents to wrap, I want to select the right wrapping paper for them. The paper can tell someone how I feel about him or her, or how I want my gift to be taken—seriously or lightheartedly. Being a person who is all thumbs when it comes to wrapping presents, I would gladly avoid the task if I could.

I'm tempted to buy some gift bags instead, shove a present in each, and be done with it. But, as much as I would enjoy the convenience of giving a gift in a bag, I have to admit that an important part of the experience gets lost with that approach, both for the recipient and for me. I love watching children tear through the ribbons and wrapping paper to get at the surprise hidden underneath, especially when I already know what the present is. And I myself enjoy the suspense of slowly unwrapping a present I've received, while giving it a careful shake to guess what might be inside.

Studying all this wrapping paper makes me reflect that unwrapping hidden things is a normal part of life. Our future, for example, is wrapped in mystery and only reveals itself with the unfolding of each new day. And every person around me is a mystery as well; I can never fully get to know someone—there is always more to be discovered. And, I suppose, this is even true when I have the courage to look deeply within myself—I'm always discovering new things about who I really am.

I'm interrupted by a woman who nudges me aside and reaches decisively for two rolls of white paper decorated with little sprigs of holly. She only took a couple of seconds to decide what she wanted, while I'm still philosophizing over the deeper meaning of wrapping paper.

I think of a line from Isaiah that we used to recite in Latin during our morning prayer: "*Vere tu es Deus absconditus*," which means "Truly, you are a God who lies hidden" (Isa. 45:15). The God of the scriptures is the greatest mystery of all and so has to constantly be a God of self-revelation, giving us glimpses into the divine nature, whether by intervening in history to rescue the Chosen People or by giving us the inspired writings of scripture. Without God's self-revelation, we would know very little about the one who loves and saves us.

The high point of God's self-revelation came, of course, at the incarnation, when the Second Person of the Blessed Trinity came among us in person, as one of us: "Veiled in flesh the Godhead see, hail th'incarnate deity!" The divine Word came to earth wrapped in human form, both revealing himself and remaining a mystery at the same time: "[Christ] emptied himself, taking the form of a slave, being born in human likeness" (Phil. 2:7–8).

Wrapping and unwrapping Christmas presents is a good way to remind ourselves of the mystery that we celebrate during this season: by becoming one of us, Jesus gives us a glimpse of the divine nature: God is love: boundless, unconditional, self-sacrificing love.

I start narrowing my choice of paper to some of the quieter designs. I like this dark green one flecked with tiny silver snowflakes. I keep thinking about God's constant self-revelation. When I pray, though, I'm always tempted to keep part of myself under wraps so as not to leave myself too vulnerable. If I let myself be totally open to God, that would mean losing control of the situation and leaving the Divine Lover in charge. I'm not quite ready for that; I'll keep some of the wrapping paper on instead.

And when I'm with other people it's the same story: it's hard to risk leaving myself completely open and vulnerable. I get so far, and then I decide to keep some of me under wraps, protected.

Finally, I decide that the dark green paper really is exactly what I need. As I reach for the roll, I think of the challenge that the divine Son gives to me at Christmas: to leave myself vulnerable and open to him and to people I love, the way he came to me in Bethlehem without the comfortable protection of wrapping paper.

Reflection

Think of some way or ways in which God has come into your life recently and revealed to you something of the divine nature. What did you learn about God?

To what extent do you leave yourself open to the Lord in your prayer, and to what extent do you hide or hold back? What about your relationships with others? Might God's self-revealing action at Christmas have a message for you with regard to either of these areas?

Sacred Scripture

Although I am the very least of all the saints, this grace was given to me to bring to the Gentiles the news of the boundless riches of Christ, and to make everyone see what is the plan of the mystery hidden for ages in God who created all things; so that through the church the wisdom of God in its rich variety might now be made known to the rulers and authorities in the heavenly places. (Eph. 3:8–10)

Rule of Benedict

If someone commits a fault while at any work—while working in the kitchen, in the storeroom, in serving, in the bakery, in the garden, in any craft or anywhere else—either by breaking or losing something or failing in any other way in any other place, he must at once come before the abbot and community and of his own accord admit his fault and make satisfaction. If it is made known through another, he is to be subjected to a more severe correction.

When the cause of the sin lies hidden in his conscience, he is to reveal it only to the abbot or to one of the spiritual elders, who know how to heal their own wounds as well as those of others, without exposing them and making them public. (Chapter 46, "Faults Committed in Other Matters," vv. 1–6)

Wednesday of the Second Week

Christmas Trees

I've just walked across the glass-enclosed pedestrian bridge that connects Newark's Penn Station with the Hilton Hotel and the Gateway One building. I pass the entrance to the deserted hotel lobby and turn right, following the corridor of shops leading away from the Hilton. At this time of the afternoon, before the rush hour, it is fairly quiet, with only an occasional businessman or woman heading for the lobby or the train. The large cube-shaped planters down the center of the corridor, which have been decorated to look like presents wrapped with red bows, form a marked contrast with the functional plain glass and aluminum store fronts lining both sides of the hallway.

Then, where the corridor makes a right angle turn to the Gateway One building, I stop in awe. Towering beneath the glass pyramid ceiling is one of the most beautiful Christmas trees I've ever seen. Every inch of it is covered with big red bows; dozens of cone-shaped ornaments in gold, silver, or green and red; and hundreds of sparkling clear white electric bulbs. Stopping to enjoy the sight, I keep noticing things I'd missed at first, such as the dozens of natural pinecones hanging from the boughs and the cluster of red bows forming a big ball at the very top of the tree.

This twelve-foot evergreen, decorated with such joy and exuberance, reminds me that the first Christmas trees symbolized the paradise tree in the

Garden of Eden and were hung with various foods and flowers. Our Christmas tree balls probably started out as apples on the tree.

I decide that I'd better get walking again, so I head for the next glass tube, which leads commuters to the Gateway Two building. As I make my way along the carpeted corridor, I keep thinking about the lovely tree and its decorations.

The Christmas tree began as a German tradition. In the 1830s, historians say, the second great wave of immigrants from Germany brought the custom of the Christmas tree with them to America. Soon all their homes and churches were decorated with Christmas trees, and before long their neighbors adopted the custom as well. It occurs to me that the Christmas tree must have arrived in America just around the time that the first Benedictines came over from Bavaria. I start to picture Father Valentine Felder and Father Eberhard Gahr arriving in Newark from Saint Vincent Archabbey in Pennsylvania to serve the German-speaking Catholics in the area and to found Saint Mary's Priory in Newark in 1857, joined shortly after by Father Rupert Seidenbusch. They must have had a Christmas tree—of course, they would have called it *ein Tannenbaum*. Every year, a few days before Christmas, the monks of Newark Abbey continue the tradition by having a party during which we sing carols as we decorate our Christmas tree in the large room just off the church.

In the sixteenth century in Germany, various Christmas traditions were combined, and the Christmas tree changed from being the paradise tree to representing Christ himself as the "tree of life." That strikes me as a great

idea: putting Christ, who came into our midst at Bethlehem, right in the middle of your living room, right where he wishes to be, in the center of your family's life.

As I make my way into the next office tower, thinking what a fine idea it is to see the Christmas tree as representing Christ, I notice another striking tree in the lobby of Gateway Two. I recently read a religious writer of the 1930s who advised believers that the Christmas tree, since it represented Christ himself, should be treated with dignity, decorated with quiet solemnity, and "kept free from any non-religious decorations of any kind." I find myself thinking how much I disagree with that narrow concept. If we say that the tree stands for Christ, then far from keeping it free from the undignified aspects of life, we should want to hang everything on it: our memories, our concerns about today, and our hopes for the future. The "Christ tree" should be able to support anything that reflects our daily lives: Disney characters, photographs of grandchildren, fire engines, and timeworn ornaments from great-grandmother.

The Christmas tree is a way of celebrating the fact that Christ came to earth and dwells among us and is at the center of my family and involved in every aspect of my life, from the most mundane to the most sublime, from the most serious to the most playful.

I've come to the end of the long corridor that now opens onto a great atrium where a gigantic white snowflake hangs against a two-story glass wall. Before getting onto the escalator, I look down and watch the pedestrians coming and going on the busy street level below. And I notice on the floor, off to one side, sparkling with white lights, yet another Christ tree. So here, I think as I get on the down escalator, how encouraging it is to see, all around this cold metal-and-glass office complex, signs that the Lord is indeed here in our midst.

Reflection

Picture an imaginary Christmas tree representing Christ at the center of your life. How would you want to decorate it? Try hanging on its branches not only your victories, the things you are most proud of, but also the faults and problems that Christ has helped you with. If you were to include pictures of people, whose pictures would you hang there first?

Sacred Scripture

You are in our midst, O Lord, your name we bear: do not forsake us! (Jer. 14:9 NAB)

Wisdom of the Desert

Abba Paul said, "Keep close to Jesus."[7]

---

7. Benedicta Ward, ed., *Daily Readings with the Fathers* (Springfield, IL: Templegate Publishers, 1990), 60.

THURSDAY OF THE
SECOND WEEK
Holiday Worries

I 'm working my way slowly upstream against the tide of oncoming shoppers on Market Street on this gray wintry afternoon. As always, I'm fascinated by the variety of faces that I see in our city: the color of skin, the texture of hair, the shape of eyes. As I start noticing faces however, I'm struck by something that many of them have in common—a preoccupied, worried look. It occurs to me that as the Christmas holidays get closer, people get busier and busier and have more things to worry about.

I've experienced this anxiety myself, even in the monastery—the extra demands of the holiday season sometimes make it hard for me to keep the peaceful and thoughtful holy days of Advent. The Greeks, I think, had a good insight when they based their word "to worry" on the verb "to divide."[8] Worrying divides our attention and our energy, sending us off in several different directions at once. Underlying the New Testament idea of "to worry," then, is the idea of "to be distracted."

As if foreseeing our twenty-first century struggle against the hectic busyness of the time before Christmas, Jesus warns us that worries can draw our attention away from watching for the day of his return: "Take heed to

---

8. The Greek *merimnao*, "to worry," is from the same root as *merizo*, "divide, split into portions."

yourselves, lest your hearts be overcome with . . . the worries of this life, and that day catch you unawares" (Luke 21:34).

Still threading my way through the crowds, I begin to imagine Jesus preaching an Advent version of the Sermon on the Mount: "Therefore I tell you, do not worry about how you will get all your shopping finished, or how the house decorations are going to get put up, or who is going to pick up grandma at the airport. Indeed your heavenly Father knows that you need all these things. Do you really think he will abandon you?" (Cf. Matt. 6:25ff). Then Isaiah chimes in with his words from this morning's mass: "For I, the Lord your God, hold your right hand; it is I who say to you, 'Do not fear, I will help you'"(Isa. 41:13). My problem is that I keep forgetting that God is offering to hold my hand and help me.

I get so wrapped up in my worries and concerns that I forget to just stop for a moment and say, "OK, Jesus, I'm getting overwhelmed. I want to hand this particular worry over to you; please take care of it as you know best." I've always found, however, that once I remember to hand my worries over to the Lord, my anxiety invariably subsides.

My musings are interrupted when I stop short to let a knot of pedestrians pass in the opposite direction, many of them carrying shopping bags. I notice one woman whose face shows both anxiety and kindness. This reminds me that there is a second kind of worrying in the New Testament that actually makes us better Christians—the anxiousness that is a natural part of loving and caring about someone. Paul tells the Philippians, for example, that he hopes to send them Timothy, who will be genuinely "anxious" for their welfare (Phil. 2:20). He tells the Corinthians that the various parts of Christ's body should worry about one another (1 Cor. 12:25). In Paul's eyes, all Christians ought to be deeply concerned—and even worried—about their brothers and sisters. This kind of worrying doesn't distract us; in fact, worrying that leads to lifting people up in prayer, commending them to God's loving care, helps us to concentrate even better on the one important thing, love.

During all the worries and distractions of the holidays, I pray I'll be able to "worry" about a certain friend who gets depressed at this time of year and a student of mine whose addicted father usually ruins Christmas for the family by abusing alcohol and drugs. If these are my worries, then, far from taking my attention away from what is truly important, they will help me focus even more on the meaning of Advent, as I pray the church's heartfelt prayer, "Come, Lord, and save your people."

I'm waiting at the light at Broad Street; almost invisible to the throngs of shoppers, a homeless man sits on a piece of cardboard rattling the change in his paper cup, hoping that some of us holiday worriers will worry about him.

Reflection

In 1 Peter 5:7 we read "Cast all your cares on the Lord." Think of one specific worry of yours that you might cast upon the Lord during the busy holiday season. Then think of someone you worry about and lift that person up to the Lord as well.

As part of your Advent preparation, ask yourself if there is perhaps someone you worry about too much. On the other hand, is there someone else for whom the Lord may want you to feel more concern than you do?

The scripture passage below, from Jesus' Sermon on the Mount, is a short treatise on worrying; the word 'worry' occurs in it six times.

Sacred Scripture

"Therefore I tell you, do not worry about your life, what you will eat or what you will drink, or about your body, what you will wear. Is not life more than food, and the body more than clothing? Look at the birds of the air; they neither sow nor reap nor gather into barns, and yet your heavenly Father feeds them. Are you not of more value than they? And can any of you by worrying add a single hour to your span of life? And why do you worry about clothing? Consider the lilies of the field, how they grow; they neither toil nor spin, yet I tell you, even Solomon in all his glory was not clothed like one of these. But if God so clothes the grass of the field, which is alive today and tomorrow is thrown into the oven, will he not much more clothe you—you of little faith? Therefore do not worry, saying, 'What will we eat?' or 'What will we drink?' or 'What will we wear?' For it is the Gentiles who strive for all these things; and indeed your heavenly Father knows that you need all these things. But strive first for the kingdom of God and his righteousness, and all these things will be given to you as well. So do not worry about tomorrow, for tomorrow will bring worries of its own. Today's trouble is enough for today." (Matt. 6:25–34)

Rule of Benedict

Great care and concern are to be shown in receiving poor people and pilgrims. (Chapter 53, "The Reception of Guests," v. 15)

Friday of the Second Week
Manger Scene

Shaking hands and trading greetings, I make my way through the dozen students who are crowding the front steps of the school at dismissal time and start down King Boulevard alongside the school building. I notice across the street, down at the corner of Springfield Avenue, that some people are standing inside the fence that runs around the gymnasium: Father Philip, the pastor of the abbey's parish church, is setting up the manger scene with the help of some parishioners.

As I walk closer to the corner, I can see that they have already erected the simple wooden stable and have placed around it big rectangular bales of straw. The statues of Mary, Joseph, and the babe are lying on the lawn waiting to be set in place.

When I stop for the light at the busy corner of Springfield Avenue, I begin to appreciate what a perfect location Father Philip has chosen for the Christmas display. Commuters on several major bus routes will pass within a few feet of it. Young people from three high schools and three nearby colleges walk past it every day. Hundreds of motorists on their way to work will see it when they stop at the traffic light.

As I'm waiting for the pedestrian signal to say walk, I start to think about Saint Francis of Assisi, who first had the idea of re-creating the scene of the poor stable in Bethlehem, including live animals. Francis said, "I want to enact the memory of the Infant who was born at Bethlehem, and how he was deprived of all the comforts babies enjoy; how he was bedded in the manger on hay, between an ass and an ox. For once I want to see all this with

46

my own eyes."[9] So on Christmas Eve in 1223, near the town of Greccio, in Italy, Francis along with a number of his brethren and a crowd of townspeople carrying torches and singing joyful songs, came in procession to that first manger display.

The light changes, and I walk across the four-lane avenue with some of my students who have come up alongside me. Arriving at the curb, I say good-bye to them as they join the people waiting for the bus; then I glance back across the wide intersection, at the manger scene. One of the parishioners is just putting the statue of Joseph in place beside the manger. As I turn and continue my walk, I begin thinking about Saint Francis' idea that the townspeople of Greccio, seeing the baby lying on the straw in the poor stable, would be reminded of Jesus' humble origins and his voluntary poverty.

Then I start to wonder what this scene on the corner means to the people who look at it every day. Do they see just another baby born, like many of Newark's babies, in obscurity and destitution? In a city burdened with a scandalous level of poverty and an infamously high rate of infant mortality, the stable seems to fit in with terrible appropriateness.

But I hope that local neighbors will be able to look at the stable scene with the eyes of Saint Francis and see something else beneath the poverty and the powerlessness: God's mysterious love unfolding in a strange and marvelous way. I hope they will be able to understand the message of the stable, a message directed particularly toward the poor and the powerless of the world: If the Messiah had been born into wealth and luxury, then poor people on the bus on the way to their low-paying jobs would have seen, on the corner of King Boulevard, a luxurious scene of a baby in an upper-class house, lying in an expensive crib and wrapped in luxurious blankets. And they might have said, "There! See! It's all about having money; that's what really counts." Or if Jesus had chosen to be born into a powerful family, perhaps as the son of the emperor in Rome, then every poor person who saw the corner display of the newborn emperor in his room in the imperial palace might have nodded his or her head, "Yup! What else do you expect? It always boils down to power! The more power you have, the happier you'll be." If the Savior had been born to a couple of world-famous celebrities, so that his baby picture was splashed on the cover of hundreds of magazines, then the anonymous homeless woman gazing through the fence at the Christmas display of the glamorous couple with their famous child could have said to

---

9. Francis X. Weiser, *Handbook of Christian Feasts and Customs* (New York: Harcourt Brace, 1952), 94–95.

herself, "Now, there's real happiness! Wish I had been born famous like that, having everybody know who I am when I walk down the street."

But the scene on the corner shows no traces of wealth, power, or fame. It portrays instead just a poor couple who had to put their baby to bed on straw and whose visitors were some scruffy shepherds from a nearby hillside. Crossing West Market Street I pray to the infant of Bethlehem that everyone who looks at Father Phil's nativity scene might see the beautiful message it bears: that the kingdom of God will be built not of power, wealth, or fame, but of humble, self-giving love—something that is within the reach of each one of us.

A young woman walks toward me holding her two-year old son by the hand, heading toward the corner nativity scene. I hope she'll stop and show him the poor baby lying on the straw.

Reflection

As you think of Jesus' choosing to be born into poverty at Bethlehem, ask yourself if there may be something which you are being called to let go of during this Advent season. Maybe new circumstances are forcing you to let go of some comfortable situation or some pleasant relationship, or perhaps age or illness is taking away a certain physical or mental ability you used to enjoy. Think of this deprivation as a share in the voluntary poverty of Jesus in Bethlehem, and offer it to him as a gift.

Sacred Scripture

> Joseph also went from the town of Nazareth in Galilee to Judea, to the city of David called Bethlehem, because he was descended from the house and family of David. He went to be registered with Mary, to whom he was engaged and who was expecting a child. While they were there, the time came for her to deliver her child. And she gave birth to her firstborn son and wrapped him in bands of cloth, and laid him in a manger, because there was no place for them in the inn. (Luke 2:4–7)

Wisdom of the Desert

Abbot Zeno, a disciple of Abbot Sylvanus, said: Do not dwell in a famous place, and do not become the disciple of a man with a great name. And do not lay any foundation when you build yourself a cell.[10]

---

10. Thomas Merton, *The Wisdom of the Desert* (New York: New Directions, 1970), 73.

SATURDAY OF THE
SECOND WEEK
Christmas Cards

I'm striding quickly up Elm Street, behind City Hall, the police head-
quarters, and the main post office, in a neighborhood where the houses
have no front yards but crowd right up to the sidewalk. I notice that in
a front window of one of the houses someone has taped five Christmas
cards, their silvers, reds, and greens standing out against the general dingi-
ness of the area.

During nice weather I sometimes see a gray-haired woman scrubbing
the cement stairs in front of this house, and I'm sure that she must have put
those cards there. I ask myself how she decided which ones to put up—

they certainly don't match
very well in size or color. Or
were these the only ones she
received? I wonder if each of
them means something spe-
cial to her.

I slow down for a closer
look. Maybe the large card
with the big Santa Claus is
from a grandchild she never
gets to see. The dark blue one
with the silver silhouette of

the virgin and child must be from her daughter or maybe from a lifelong friend. Not wishing to be impolite by staring at the window, I keep moving along without getting a good look at the other cards.

I start thinking about my own relatives and friends who use Christmas cards to stay in touch with me each year. I especially enjoy the ones with the latest family photograph on the front, showing all the kids dressed in red sweaters and looking a year older.

As I get near the corner, I can see directly ahead, on the other side of Mulberry Street, a pair of tractor trailers parked at the loading docks behind the main post office, loading and unloading tons of Christmas mail. I think of the basket of Christmas cards in the monastery's community room and how I enjoy thumbing through them to see who is thinking of us during these holy days. I usually read the long single-spaced family chronicles that a few alumni include with their cards to find out how they and their families are doing.

Crossing toward the loading docks of the post office now, I start thinking of the thousands of Christmas cards being processed and sorted inside. Suddenly I remember some lines from a poem by Walt Whitman: "I see something of God each hour of the twenty-four, and each moment then, . . . I find letters from God dropt in the street, and every one is signed by God's name."[11]

I've always liked that image of letters from God dropped at our feet. It reminds me of Saint Benedict's conviction that God is everywhere and is always trying to communicate with us, waiting for us to listen attentively and look carefully.

OK, then, I ask myself: has God dropped any letters at my feet recently? I think right away of the children at mass last Sunday and how their smiles made me feel so close to the Lord. And then there was the Christmas card I received yesterday from a young couple whose wedding I witnessed last spring; along with the card, they enclosed a snapshot of the wedding ceremony. I smiled when I saw that picture—it was definitely a Christmas card from God. And what about that compliment from a colleague after my presentation at the faculty meeting this morning? Maybe even losing my temper in class yesterday was a letter from God, since it told me clearly that I need to relax a little and stop taking myself so seriously.

During this time of year we can get so busy that we forget to look for the Christmas cards the Lord has "dropt in the street" for us. I wonder: how many have I unknowingly rushed past just this week?

---

11. Walt Whitman, "Song of Myself," in *Leaves of Grass*, stanza 48, line 18.

At the corner now, I have to wait for a mail truck to rumble out of the parking lot before I can cross Mulberry Street. As I reach the other side, I notice a well-dressed man get out of a double-parked car on Green Street and walk briskly to the sidewalk mail box, carrying two big fistfuls of white envelopes. They're not business envelopes, though; they look more like Christmas cards. I watch as he opens the little door on the top of the mailbox and tosses them in. With his Christmas cards on their way, he turns and, with an air of satisfaction, strides back to his car and drives off. And it occurs to me that God must entrust me with the task of delivering many of those divine Christmas cards to others: a little favor done for a brother monk, spending fifteen minutes listening to a student tell me his problems, taking special care to prepare a good homily for the people for whom I say mass on Sunday. God uses me to drop all of these "letters" at people's feet to assure them that they are loved, and that the Lord is with them every minute.

As I watch people going in and out of the post office, I decide that I had better be looking for Christmas cards from the Lord in the people and events around me—"letters from God dropt in the street, and every one is signed by God's name."

Reflection

Think of one or two ways in which God has "dropped a letter at your feet" recently. Did you recognize it right away? Was its message a welcome one? How did you respond to it? When has the Lord used you to deliver a message of love and concern to someone?

Sacred Scripture

Long ago God spoke to our ancestors in many and various ways by the prophets, but in these last days he has spoken to us by a Son, whom he appointed heir of all things, through whom he also created the worlds. He is the reflection of God's glory and the exact imprint of God's very being, and he sustains all things by his powerful word. (Heb. 1:1–3)

Wisdom of the Desert

A certain philosopher asked St. Antony: Father, how can you be so happy when you are deprived of the consolation of books? Antony replied: "My book, O philosopher, is the nature of created things, and any time I want to read the words of God, the book is before me."[12]

---

12. Thomas Merton, *The Wisdom of the Desert* (New York: New Directions, 1970), 62.

SUNDAY OF THE THIRD WEEK
Joy

I've just concelebrated Sunday mass in Saint Mary's, the abbey's parish church, and now I'm standing outside in the brisk wind, greeting the parishioners. I begin to shake hands and say hello to everyone along the sidewalk. Since the majority of these parishioners are from West Africa, their colorful clothes dominate the scene even from beneath their winter coats: the women in long turquoise and silver skirts and tall head-wraps, the men in wide-legged trousers and dashikis. The vivid colors and the shouted greetings make for an appropriately joyful scene on this particular day. This is the Third Sunday of Advent, traditionally called *Gaudete* Sunday, "Rejoice Sunday," celebrating the fact that we are now halfway through Advent. The readings and chants at mass invite us to reflect on the Christian gift of joy.

"Joy" is one of the most familiar of our "season's greetings." We repeat it on our Christmas cards and decorations and in our carols. It is no accident that "joy" has become a traditional part of holiday greetings. In the New Testament, the rejoicing begins even before Jesus is born. Words based on the root verb "be joyful"[13] appear several times in the opening lines of Luke's infancy narrative. The angel Gabriel announces to Zechariah the birth of John the Baptist with the promise: "And you will have joy and gladness, and will rejoice at his birth" (Luke 1:14). Then there is the angel's greeting to Mary: "Hail [literally "Rejoice"] highly favored one" (Luke 1:28). Then the angel of the Lord announces to the shepherds (in a literal

---

13. Greek *chairō*, "rejoice, be glad;" *chara*, "joy, delight;" *charitoō*, "favor someone."

translation), "Behold, I proclaim to you a great joy that will be for all the people" (Luke 2:10).

Matthew tells us that when the star that the magi had been following came to a stop over the place where the child was, the wise men literally "rejoiced with joy" (Matt. 2:10). Jesus will continue to be a source of joy to others throughout his public life, as he announces the kingdom and performs miracles.

While I'm now chatting with a young couple from the parish, suddenly, their little one-year-old in her stroller lets out a shriek of delight. We all laugh as we watch her wave her tiny fists in the air. She doesn't seem to be responding to anything in particular; she's just delighting in being alive and doesn't know how better to express it at the moment.

Her shout of joy makes me think of a brief clip from a home video that has recently become so much of a pop-culture phenomenon that it is used in a television commercial. The video shows two children in pajamas opening their Christmas presents. As a young boy peels the gold wrapping paper from his parents' gift, his face lights up: "Nintendo 64! Oh, my God!" His screams and the repeated shouts of "Thank you!" from his younger sister go on for at least a minute of unmitigated joy that their father captured on home video. This child's reaction to a Nintendo game is a perfect picture of overwhelming joy.

Although the New Testament word for joy usually refers to "calm delight," there are times when it makes people throw their hands in the air and shout. This is the case with the man who discovers a treasure: "The kingdom of heaven is like a treasure buried in a field, which a person finds and hides again, and out of joy goes and sells all that he has and buys that field" (Matt. 13:44). His deep, powerful joy makes him forget himself, let go of everything else, and accept the kingdom with all his heart.

I look again at the baby in her stroller; now she's quietly taking in the whole busy scene: laughter, conversations, car horns honking as people cut across King Boulevard in the middle of the block.

At the climax of the gospel story, when the women are told by an angel on Easter morning that Jesus has been raised from the dead, they leave the grave filled with great joy (Matt. 28:8). Later that same day the risen Lord appears to the apostles and shows them his hands and his side. At this point, John writes in a masterpiece of understatement, "The disciples rejoiced when they saw the Lord" (John 20:20). Finally, in the very last sentence of Luke's gospel, the disciples, after watching Jesus ascend into heaven, "returned to Jerusalem with great joy" (Luke 24:52).

The joy, then, starts even before the angel Gabriel is sent from heaven to Mary, and it is still going on after Jesus has ascended back to the Father. And so the gospel narrative ends as it began, on a note of joy.

Watching the parishioners laughing and chatting in front of the church, I start to wonder why our Christian saints are often pictured as glum and unsmiling and why some of today's most outspoken defenders of Christian values come across as grim and cheerless. It's almost as if a long face were the first prerequisite for being a follower of Christ. This is completely contrary to the spirit of joy that we find in the prophets who foretell the coming of the Messiah and in the gospel writers' accounts of the birth of the Savior.

My mass vestments are providing little protection from the cold, so I decide I had better get back inside. I wave to the baby in her stroller and say good-bye to a few more people as I make my way up the steps and into the church. I smile as I think about the baby girl's cry of joy and the unbridled joy of those two children in the video, a beautiful way to begin Gaudete Sunday, the joyful midpoint of Advent.

Reflection

Think of someone you know who radiates Christian joy. What is it about that person that makes you think of him or her as joyful? Think of some ways you might show that same joy to others during this holy season.

Sacred Scripture

For the kingdom of God is not a matter of food and drink, but of righteousness, peace, and joy in the Holy Spirit. (Rom. 14:17)

Rule of Benedict

But as we progress in this way of life and in faith, we shall run on the path of God's commandments, our hearts overflowing with the inexpressible delight of love. (Prologue, v. 49)

MONDAY OF THE THIRD WEEK[14]
Home for the Holidays

I have a little extra time today, so I'm taking a long walk across the Passaic River and through the town of Harrison. I turn down a narrow street toward the brand-new housing development made up of dozens of brick townhouses, most of them four stories high. I start following the new sidewalk among the recently finished houses, not quite sure where it will take me. As I walk along, I notice signs that the first residents have moved in. There are several cars parked in the street, for example, and a small wreath on a front door. Then I see evergreen roping wound along the bright white railing of a second-floor porch; someone is already transforming their new house into a home.

Continuing down the block, I start thinking how Christmas time makes us more aware of our homes. We clean them, decorate them, and welcome people into them. Millions of people visit "home" during the holidays because home is the scene of many of their happiest memories, and it is the place to reconnect with family. Most of us spend a lot of time, money, and effort preparing our homes to welcome family and friends.

"Home" surely had a special significance for certain early Christians because, before there were church buildings, the community would gather in their houses for worship. This would have seemed quite natural to Jewish converts to Christianity—for Jews, the home was indeed the primary

---

14. For the reflections for Dec. 17 through Dec. 24, see pages 77 through 101.

place of worship, and the family was the center of religious life. So it was that certain Christians' homes became centers for the church community. Paul mentions a couple of such places: "Aquila and Prisca, together with the church in their house, send you hearty greetings in the Lord" (1 Cor. 16:19, cf. Rom 16:5). "Give my greetings to the brethren at Laodicea, and to Nympha and the church in her house" (Col. 4:15). For Christians, then, the original "sacred spaces" were not basilicas, cathedrals, or chapels, but their own homes.

We modern Christians, too, would do well to see our own homes as sacred places where we encounter God in the love of our families and friends, in quiet moments of rest, and even in the struggles with illness and disappointments. When we enter our houses, we ought to hear the Lord saying to us the same thing he said to Moses who was approaching the divine presence in the burning bush: "Remove the sandals from your feet, for the place on which you are standing is holy ground" (Exod. 3:5).

I'm nearing the end of the area of these newly finished houses, and I notice a few more parked cars and a child's tricycle on a lawn. Ahead of me, a dozen more houses are in various stages of construction, some close to completion, with blank white sheets of plastic covering the window openings. I imagine that there are people already waiting impatiently to move in and start to make these lifeless buildings into homes.

As I think of the families preparing for the first holidays in their new homes, expecting visits from relatives, another New Testament image of home comes to mind. In the Letter to the Ephesians Paul tells the gentiles, "So then you are no longer strangers and sojourners, but you are fellow citizens with the saints and members of the household of God" (Eph. 2:19; cf. Heb. 3:5–6). Although it's an image that occurs several times in the New Testament, I suddenly realize that I've never thought of myself as a member of "the household of God." I start to think about it. For me, *household* evokes a feeling of closeness, security, and warmth, a place where I am accepted and loved for who I am.

It seems to me, though, that this "household of God" sounds awfully abstract and terribly unwieldy. But then I start to name the people I know who belong to it: my brother monks, my family, my friends, my students. The circle starts expanding quickly and easily: my favorite cousin, whom I seldom get to see; certain friends in Europe; the parishioners in Fatima parish in Santa Cruz, Bolivia. Only then do I start to think of the millions of people I've never met but who share my faith, who read the same scriptures, who pray with the same emotions as I do. Now the household doesn't seem so forbiddingly abstract.

I'm now walking on the rough blacktop in front of the newest houses, which are still just empty shells, lifeless, dark, and cold, but I'm warmed by the memories of my own home during the holidays and by my newly discovered sense of belonging to God's own household.

Reflection

Reflect on your home as a sacred place in which you encounter the Lord. Take a few minutes to name the various ways in which you meet God there: relaxing with family members, sharing meals, praying, and so on. What might you do during Advent to make you and your family members more aware of this sacredness?

What might you do during Advent to celebrate your membership in the wider household of God, the church?

Sacred Scripture

So then you are no longer strangers and sojourners, but you are fellow citizens with the holy ones and members of the household of God, built upon the foundation of the apostles and prophets, with Christ Jesus himself as the capstone. . . . In him you also are being built together into a dwelling place of God in the Spirit. (Eph. 2:19–20, 22 NAB)

Wisdom of Saint Athanasius

"[Antony] after journeying three days and three nights into the desert, came to a very high hill. Below the hill there was water—perfectly clear, sweet and quite cold, and beyond there were plains, and a few untended date palms. Then Antony, as if stirred by God, fell in love with the place. . . . Looking on it as his own home, from that time forward he stayed in that place." *(The Life of Antony)*[15]

---

15. Robert C. Gregg, trans. and intro., *Athanasius: The Life of Antony and the Letter to Marcellinus* (Mahwah, NJ: Paulist Press, 1980), 68.

TUESDAY OF THE THIRD WEEK[16]
Peace On Earth?

"Father Albert?"

At the sound of a woman's voice calling my name I stop on the wide sidewalk in front of City Hall. Turning around I recognize the mother of one of my students.

"Hi!" I answer. "How are you, Mrs. Parker? All ready for Christmas?"

"Father, I don't even want to think about it! There's just too much to do, what with shopping for presents, cleaning the house, decorating and what-not—and still going to work every day!"

"I hear you, ma'am!" I respond in hurried politeness. "And it's so crowded downtown that I have to stay on the side streets if I want to take a walk. Well, listen, I don't want to hold you up. I hope you get all your shopping done. And have a good Christmas."

"Thanks; same to you, Father." She stares at me, slightly perplexed, I think, at my cutting the conversation short. But I have a lot of things to do.

As I continue along Broad Street, I reach into my pocket and pull out my "Palm Pilot," my electronic calendar and planner. I punch up my to-do list: hang up the garlands in the monastery refectory, print up the programs for Thursday's Christmas Program, prepare the music for this afternoon's community's mass, return a bunch of emails. . . . The list, unfortunately, doesn't all fit on one screen, but I don't have the courage to scroll down to

---

16. For the reflections for Dec. 17 through Dec. 24, see pages 77 through 101.

look at the rest of it. That would just make me more stressed. With a sigh, I turn it off, shove it back into my pocket, and keep walking. Even in a quiet monastery there seem to be so many things to do before Christmas that I have to work at staying calm and peaceful.

Over the front door of the monastery is the Latin motto "*Pax,*" "Peace." This is not an advertisement for what things are actually like inside the cloister; rather, peace is our goal. Peace, Benedict says, should be our aim, something we work at full time in the monastery. And, as anyone who has ever lived in a community can tell you, peace is not always easy to come by. Our goal is not a total absence of stress or an idyllic life free from difficulties. Instead, what we work at achieving as individuals and as a community is what someone has aptly called "peace under pressure." This is what I'm working on during this third week of Advent: staying peaceful while checking things off of my long to-do list.

As I make my way toward Market Street, I notice a woman climbing onto the number 13 bus with four huge shopping bags from the toy store. As she wrestles them through the door and up the steep steps, I notice that she looks angry and frustrated. But in those bags there are probably gifts that she chose carefully for some children she loves deeply.

The loud honk of a horn startles me; halfway across Branford Place, I look quickly to my right, where a car with a Christmas tree tied to its roof is pushing into the pedestrians in the crosswalk as if resentful of their presence. I keep walking towards the other curb, wishing that I could tell that driver and that woman with the shopping bags a couple of Saint Benedict's hints for finding peace under pressure.

One great help toward keeping a sense of peace and joy in the midst of rushing around is to cultivate a sense of true humility: when I admit that I am not God, then I no longer expect to be able to accomplish everything that I want, or to control every event or person around me. Humility can take a lot of the pressure off.

Benedict offers another important way to find peace in the hectic busyness of the holidays: remembering that what you do is not as important as how you do it. Benedict says, for example, that external obedience does not count if it is performed with an ill will. This principle was a real help to me some years ago. I had the stressful job every summer of writing the school's master schedule and making up and revising students' schedules for September. After some years of being very stressed by this task, it suddenly occurred to me to look more closely at why I was doing all that work. I realized that I was doing it not to beat deadlines or to master a challenge, but because it was my own unique way of loving. I began to see those endless hours of problem-solving and list-making as my gift to everyone in the school community, from administrators and teachers to parents and students—especially students. Once I came to realize this, the work was still there, and the deadlines still loomed; but I had changed: I was no longer struggling to master the task; I was working in order to give a gift to the members of my community.

Back in the midst of Advent, and keeping in mind the principle of the importance of our interior motivation, we can think of hectic Christmas shopping as a way of loving the people for whom we're buying gifts. We could consciously cultivate this same attitude toward our other holiday tasks as well, whether decorating, cooking, or printing copies of music; they could become not just challenges to be conquered or so many stressful projects with deadlines, but rather, special ways of loving our family and friends.

The pressure will still be there, but so will a certain peace of heart that comes from living a life of self-giving love. And how better to prepare for Christ's coming than all these ways of showing our love for others?

I find myself barely able to walk in the crush of people at the corner of Broad and Market. I can sense the stress in the people around me and, yes, plenty of love as well.

Reflection

Are there things that you have to do during the holidays which you usually look at as being done out of love? Think of some holiday task or obligation you do not particularly enjoy, and try looking at it as something you do out of love for others.

Sacred Scripture

"Come to me, all you that are weary and are carrying heavy burdens, and I will give you rest. Take my yoke upon you, and learn from me; for I am gentle and humble in heart, and you will find rest for your souls. For my yoke is easy, and my burden is light." (Matt. 11:28–30)

Rule of Benedict

God then directs these words to you: If you desire true and eternal life, keep your tongue free from vicious talk and your lips from all deceit; turn away from evil and do good; let peace be your quest and aim. (Prologue, v. 17)

WEDNESDAY OF THE THIRD WEEK[17]

Santa Claus

I'm enjoying the unusually mild afternoon and the cloudless blue sky as I stroll up Lafayette Street in the Ironbound neighborhood. The houses are uniformly small and crowded together, with narrow alleyways between. When a flash of red catches my eye, I turn to see, on the slanted roof of a house across the street, a plastic Santa Claus four feet tall, complete with his sleigh and eight reindeer.

17. For the reflections for Dec. 17 through Dec. 24, see pages 77 through 101.

I immediately remember the magical watercolor illustrations of Santa in a children's edition of Clement Clarke Moore's *A Visit from Saint Nicholas*. As a little child I never got tired of hearing or reading that poem and climbing inside those painted scenes; the words and the pictures are still vivid memories after all these years: "'Twas the night before Christmas, and all through the house. . . . " That poem is one of my fondest and most vivid associations with Christmas, and I can still recite most of the words by heart.

A large truck rumbles by; on its side is a six-foot high face of a smiling Santa Claus winking and wishing everyone "Season's Greetings" from a supermarket chain. Earlier today I was reading how our present Santa Claus evolved from several figures, among them the fourth-century bishop, Saint Nicholas, and the English Father Christmas, and even the German god Thor, who, it seems, was often pictured as a jovial, friendly, and rotund fellow with a long white beard. In the early 1930s, when images of Santa Claus were further popularized through Haddon Sundblom's depiction of him for the Coca-Cola Company's Christmas advertising, Santa Claus soon became the best known and most beloved of all the holiday figures.

My idea of Santa Claus, however, is forever bound up with my favorite lines from that poem:

As I drew in my head, and was turning around,
Down the chimney Saint Nicholas came with a bound.

It makes perfect sense that Saint Nicholas, the patron saint of children, should have the role of bringing presents.

Now, as I pass the playground of Saint James School, an orange brick building from the 1950s that replaced the old Saint James Hospital building where I was born, I watch some young boys kicking a soccer ball across the blacktop behind the high chain-link fence.

But I keep thinking about those figures that combined to form our Santa Claus: Father Christmas, Thor, Kris Kringle, and Saint Nicholas. Saint Nicholas, who lived in what is now Turkey, known for his kindness to the poor, was one of the most beloved saints of the Middle Ages. The legends tell of his generosity to the needy, including the time he secretly provided money to a family whose daughters could not get married because their father couldn't afford their dowries. I particularly like the stories of his dropping bags of gold down chimneys, and, a favorite subject for religious artists, throwing bags of gold through open windows where they landed in the stockings that had been hung by the fireplace to dry. I once read that there are more paintings of Saint Nicholas in medieval Christian art than of any other saint.

When saints went out of fashion in many countries at the time of the Protestant Reformation, Saint Nicholas' feast was abolished, along with the celebrations of all the other saints' days. Yet, the Dutch, among whom were many Catholics, held onto the feast of Saint Nicholas and the custom of giving gifts to children on that day. When they came to New Amsterdam (old New York City), not ten miles from where I'm walking right now, they brought with them the custom of celebrating, each December sixth, the traditional visit from Saint Nicholas, whom they called Sinter Klaas. After the Dutch were driven out of New Amsterdam, it seems that the children of the British colonists must have prevailed on their parents to continue the custom of giving gifts to children. But Sinter Klaas, evolving into Santa Claus, no longer had his own feast day and had to bring his presents on Christmas day.

Sadly, Santa Claus has come to represent the secular, consumerist side of the Christmas season, distracting many of us from Jesus, the true center of the feast, and, ironically, focusing our children not on Saint Nicholas' generous giving but on greedy present-getting. The commercialized figure of Santa Claus portrayed in plastic roof figures and on sides of trucks seems to have little to do with the saintly bishop Nicholas, but underneath all the layers of marketing and advertising gimmicks, however, Santa will always be Saint Nicholas, Bishop of Myra, who loved children and who tossed bags of gold through poor people's windows.

I keep up my pace, enjoying the signs of approaching Christmas in people's windows—electric candles, colored lights, and evergreen wreaths. As I pass the end of the playground, and the shouts of the soccer players start to fade, I say a quick prayer to Saint Nicholas asking him to watch over the children and the poor of our city. I finish my prayer and then notice on someone's front door a larger-than-life plastic face of a smiling Santa Claus—I mean, Saint Nicholas.

Reflection

If Saint Nicholas imitated Christ's self-giving by being good to the poor and the needy, how are you called to do the same in your life? Is there some particular person or group you might be called to help during this holy season? How might you be called to imitate Saint Nicholas, not just during the holidays but throughout the year?

Sacred Scripture

People were bringing little children to him in order that he might touch them; and the disciples spoke sternly to them. But when Jesus saw this, he was indignant and said to them, "Let the little children come to me; do not stop them; for it is to such as these that the kingdom of God belongs. Truly I tell you, whoever does not receive the kingdom of God as a little child will never enter it." And he took them up in his arms, laid his hands on them, and blessed them. (Mark 10:13–16)

Rule of Benedict

You must relieve the lot of the poor, clothe the naked, visit the sick, and bury the dead. Go to help the troubled and console the sorrowing. (Chapter 4, "The Tools for Good Works," vv. 14–19)

Thursday of the Third Week[18]

Looking for the Right Gift

The wide corridor of Pennsylvania Station in Newark is almost deserted at this hour. Running parallel to the main hallway, it only comes to life during the morning and evening rush hours. Parked in a long row down the center of its marble floors are vendors' carts offering leather goods, scarves, gloves, jewelry, and African art. As I stroll past one of the carts, I notice a woman absent-mindedly flipping through a pile of colored gloves. Facing her across the cart is another woman who has a whole different attitude: she's clearly searching for something. I can tell by the look of concentration in her eyes that she knows exactly what she's looking for and will surely know it when she sees it. She lifts a pair of red gloves, studies the label and the price tag for a moment, then puts it down and continues sorting methodically through the rest of the pile.

As I walk on past the woman who is hunting for gloves, I think about how often Sacred Scripture and the Christian spiritual tradition talk about "seeking God," "searching for Ultimate Meaning," and "finding salvation." Jesus, for example, tells the story of a merchant looking for fine pearls who, one day, finds the pearl of great price (Matt. 13:45). In Acts, Saint Paul tells the Greeks in Athens that God created the nations "so that they would search for God—and perhaps grope for him and find him—though indeed he is

---

18. For the reflections for Dec. 17 through Dec. 24, see pages 77 through 101.

not far from each one of us" (Acts 17:27). Indeed, St. Benedict in his *Rule for Monks* makes "seeking God" the monk's main task in life, and wants the community to test the would-be novice "to see if he truly seeks God" (RB 58:7).

Suddenly I'm picturing an old sight gag from the movies. The terrified Abbot and Costello are tiptoeing single file through a dark haunted house, eyes wide with fright, staring straight ahead in search of the monster. Soon the very ghoul they are looking for shuffles up behind them unnoticed, following his pursuers with hands poised threateningly over their heads.

I reach the end of the wide corridor, smiling at the picture of Bud and Lou searching in the dark while being pursued by the very thing they're hunting for. But it occurs to me that this scene is a perfect image of the basic question built into everyone's quest for God, namely, when all is said and done, who is seeking whom?

If there are biblical passages that encourage us to seek God or the kingdom, there are even more in which God is doing the searching and not us. Ezekiel compares God to a shepherd: "For thus says the Lord God: I myself will search for my sheep, and will seek them out. As shepherds seek out their flocks when they are among their scattered sheep, so I will seek out my sheep" (Ezek. 34:11). Jesus takes up this same image in his parable of the lost sheep (Luke 15:4–7).

At the very beginning of the *Holy Rule*, Saint Benedict, so famous for his emphasis on seeking God, presents the Lord as looking for us: "Seeking his workman in a multitude of people, the Lord calls out to him and lifts his voice again: is there anyone here who yearns for life and desires to see good days?" (RB Prologue, vv. 14–15).

In the same period during which Christmas shopping finds us searching, seeking, looking for exactly the right gifts to give, Advent celebrates the world's longing, humanity's search for God. I start singing to myself the words of the carol,

> Oh holy night! The stars are brightly shining,
> It is the night of the dear Saviour's birth.
> Long lay the world in sin and error pining . . .

But wait a minute! Who is pining for whom? Christmas is not about our pining for God, it's about God's pining for us so intensely and passionately that He takes on our flesh and comes to walk among us.

An image flashes into my mind: that woman at the cart searching so intently for the right pair of gloves. When my restless seeking for the Lord seems to be in vain, and I begin to get discouraged, I can think of her. But instead of thinking that she stands for me, I can see that she is even more like God, the One who is constantly, relentlessly, and lovingly searching for me.

As I turn right at the end of the side corridor and stride toward the rear door of the station, I nearly get bowled over by the flood of commuters rushing into the station—it's the start of rush hour. Men and women in business dress and others in work uniforms charge down the hallway as if they are pursuing something. A good reminder that in my earnest "search for God" I sometimes need to stand still and wait in joyful hope until the Lord finds me.

Reflection

In your relationship with God, do you see yourself more often as the seeker or the one being sought? What are some ways in which you seek God? Think of some ways in which God may have been seeking you lately. What do you think you might need to change during these holy days in order to allow the Lord to catch up with you?

Sacred Scripture

In the morning, while it was still very dark, he got up and went out to a deserted place, and there he prayed. And Simon and his companions hunted for him. When they found him, they said to him, "Everyone is searching for you." (Mark 1:35–37)

Rule of Benedict

Seeking his workman in a multitude of people, the Lord calls out to him and lifts his voice again: is there anyone here who yearns for life and desires to see good days? (Prologue, vv. 14–15)

FRIDAY OF THE THIRD WEEK[19]
Holiday Crowds

I'm walking with a friend along West Fiftieth Street in Manhattan. We're using the south side of the street to avoid the long line of people standing on the sidewalk alongside Radio City Music Hall waiting to get in to see the Christmas show. Even this side, though, is getting more and more crowded as we get closer to Rockefeller Center. Up ahead we can see dozens of people spilling onto the street, and darting back and forth between parked cars.

For most of us, whether we like them or not, crowds are part of the holiday experience. We meet them in the mall, at Christmas programs, and even at midnight mass.

As my friend and I get nearer to the cross street that forms one side of Rockefeller Center, we start to hear Christmas music, and moments later we're standing at the edge of a sea of people that fills the wide space known as Rockefeller Plaza. The center of attention is a block away, at the other end of the Plaza—a ninety-foot Christmas tree with thirty thousand colored lights. We cross West Fiftieth Street and start to make our way slowly toward the tree.

Although there is barely space to move one step at a time, no one really seems to mind; they are caught up in the contagious, festive mood, an atmosphere of celebration. We pass alongside wire-sculpted herald angels with

---

19. For the reflections for Dec. 17 through Dec. 24, see pages 77 through 101.

their golden trumpets, past parents gripping little children firmly by the hand or pushing strollers; past senior citizens, high school students, and stylishly dressed yuppies, all crowded together with thousands of others. We have all come to see the tree and enjoy the festive atmosphere of Rockefeller Plaza at Christmas time.

As we get closer to the tree, I glance to my right and glimpse, at the far end of a wide passageway between two buildings, a corner of Saint Patrick's Cathedral on Fifth Avenue. There will be crowds there today, too, lined up to get in for a peek at the historic gothic church and the elaborate nativity scene set up in the back.

Suddenly, I almost bump into a man who turns to me and asks, "Would you mind taking our picture?" He nods toward his family standing with their backs to the beautiful tree. I oblige, trying to include the bright star on the top. Even through the viewfinder their wide smiles blend beautifully with the lights on the tree.

We finally get to the edge of the sunken ice rink near the base of the tree and look down onto a glowing white world where skaters of all sizes, shapes, and abilities skate in a great clockwise circle to the Christmas music pouring from the speakers. Some are dancing gracefully, gliding backwards and showing off with elegant loops and spirals; others are barely managing to stay upright. Two little children, a boy and a girl, hold hands tightly as they take choppy baby steps along the side wall.

I turn away from the ice skaters and realize that I've lost my friend in the crowd. Nothing to panic over, but it could take quite a while to find him again in this throng. Luckily, I spot him just a few steps away and walk over to join him.

"Isn't this crowd unbelievable?" I comment.

He answers, "Yeah. It's great. But to tell you the truth, I could do without all these people. I don't like crowds."

I think to myself that, even if you dislike crowds, it's hard to avoid being caught up in the spirit of celebration here. Maybe this was what it felt like in the enthusiastic, shouting throngs that followed Jesus. I hear snatches of conversations in several different languages, reminding me that people come from all over the world to enjoy the Christmas tree and the exciting atmosphere at Rockefeller Plaza.

Suddenly, I remember that all during Advent we have been preparing for Christ's second coming at the end of time, and I recall Saint John describing it in his vision: "After this I looked, and there was a great multitude that no one could count, from every nation, from all tribes and peoples and languages, standing before the throne and before the Lamb, robed in white, with palm branches in their hands. They cried out in a loud voice, saying, 'Salvation belongs to our God who is seated on the throne, and to the Lamb'" (Rev. 7:9–10)! These are the elect, who have survived suffering and even martyrdom through the merits of Christ, the Lamb who was sacrificed to redeem the world.

Standing in this crowd, I start to think of all the struggles and sorrows, sufferings and trials that these people, including me, live with, and then I rejoice at the thought that one day, when all our sufferings are behind us, we will all be part of the countless white-robed throng singing God's praises in heaven. We will have come from all the corners of the—

"Well, I guess I've seen enough; how about you?" My friend's broad hint jolts me back into the present. He continues, "You ready to go over to Saint Patrick's?"

But I really don't want to leave. Not yet. I'm just starting to enjoy this little foretaste of heaven.

Reflection

Reflect on Saint John's image of heaven: "a great multitude that no one could count, from every nation, from all tribes and peoples and languages, standing before the throne and before the Lamb" (Rev. 7:9). Put yourself into that scene for a moment. Imagine the sounds, feel the press of the people around you, try to sense the joy of the millions of white-robed "saints."

Think about one of the various crowds you may encounter during the holidays: at a concert, for example, or at a shopping mall, or even in church. Reflect on these facts: each person in that crowd is personally known and loved by God, and each of them is likely to wind up in that heavenly throng with you. In that world there will be no more walls of fear or animosity to separate us from one another. Look into your own heart for any walls that you may have placed there, which separate you from certain individuals or groups, and remember that at the coming of our Lord, those walls will come down to make way for the single white-robed throng. Think of a specific thing you might do during this holy season to start breaking down one of those walls ahead of time.

Sacred Scripture

Then I looked, and I heard the voice of many angels surrounding the throne and the living creatures and the elders; they numbered myriads of myriads and thousands of thousands, singing with full voice, 'Worthy is the Lamb that was slaughtered to receive power and wealth and wisdom and might and honor and glory and blessing!" (Rev. 5:11–12)

Wisdom of the Desert

Saint John Kolovos, one of the greatest Fathers of the Egyptian Skete [desert] said: "It is not possible to build a house by beginning from the top, but the structure must be begun from the foundation and built up to the roof." When asked what the foundation meant, he replied: "The foundation is our neighbor. We must win him and begin with him. On him are based all the commandments of Christ."[20]

---

20. Bishop Ignatius Brianchaninov, *The Arena: An Offering to Contemporary Monasticism* (Madras: Diocesan Press, 1970), 60.

Sunday of the Fourth Week
Act Now!

Striding down Springfield Avenue, I glance at the window of the furniture store. Taped to the inside of the plate glass is a copy of the store's full-page newspaper ad proclaiming "Final Week of our Holiday Blowout Sale!" The rest of the sheet is filled with black-and-white photographs of bedroom sets, sofas, and dining room tables, each with a price printed next to it. As I continue past the store, I think about the dire warnings that merchants have been issuing lately: "Only five days left 'til Christmas!" "Act now before it's too late!" Then I start hearing the church's urgent Advent warnings: "Now is the time to rise from sleep" and "The kingdom is at Hand!" The voices if Isaiah, the storekeepers, John the Baptist, and the mail order merchants all blend together in a single chorus: "Get ready! It's closer than you think! Don't get caught unawares."

Certainly John the Baptist's familiar cry, "Repent, for the kingdom of heaven is at hand" (Matt. 3:2), helps to heighten the sense of expectation as we get closer to Christmas. But the tone of John's warning is very different from that of the advertisers' claim that time is running out: the translation "is at hand" misses a crucial point. When John says "the kingdom is at hand," the Greek verb "to be at hand" is in the past tense—the action is already completed. He is not forecasting some future event but is saying the kingdom has already arrived.[21] No store is going to run an advertisement that

---

21. The NRSV translation reflects this with "Repent, for the kingdom of heaven has come near" (Matt 3:2 NRSV).

reads, "Christmas is here. It arrived this morning," since by then it is too late for shoppers to do much about it. But that's what John's message sounds like in the original: "The kingdom has arrived." There is no time left for thinking things through or for getting used to the idea of possibly committing ourselves. The message demands an immediate, decisive response.

As I look at the dozen people waiting at the bus stop, I remember that the French philosopher Blaise Pascal writes somewhere that the problem with Christians is that we spend our entire lives waiting, getting ready for something, and so we never become people of action. That sounds like me. Since I usually prefer the prudent, cautious, gradual approach to life, I don't throw myself into a project without first looking ahead and evaluating my various options and looking at the possible consequences. This is especially true in my relationship with God. I'm still getting ready to let God take over—I'm calculating first what it will actually cost me. But John's use of the past tense ought to shock me out of my cautious, calculating mode and into instant action. The reign of God stares at me every day in the eyes of students who make demands on me; it calls out to me in the voice of a friend who needs me to act out of selfless love, and it challenges me in the quiet insistence of my conscience or in the uncompromising words of the gospels.

As the next bus pulls up at the stop, I notice a large advertisement posted along its side, warning shoppers that, soon, a certain holiday sale will be over. It doesn't sound as urgent as the cry of John the Baptist, I think to myself, but it's still a good reminder: the kingdom is already here.

Reflection

Read the account of the preaching of John the Baptist in Matthew 3:1–12 (the first three verses of which are cited in the scripture section that follows). Try to feel the urgency of the past tense of "to draw near" in the expression "the kingdom has already appeared in your midst!" Let it give you a more urgent attitude toward some difficult decision you have been putting off or some change you need to make.

Sacred Scripture

In those days John the Baptist appeared in the wilderness of Judea, proclaiming, "Repent, for the kingdom of heaven has come near." This is the one of whom the prophet Isaiah spoke when he said,

"The voice of one crying out in the wilderness: 'Prepare the way of the Lord, make his paths straight.'" (Matt. 3:1–3)

Rule of Benedict

Let us get up then, at long last, for the scriptures rouse us when they say: It is high time for us to arise from sleep. Let us open our eyes to the light that comes from God, and our ears to the voice from heaven that every day calls out this charge: If you hear his voice today, do not harden your hearts. (Prologue, vv. 8–10)

DECEMBER 17
Poinsettias

As I'm walking along Ferry Street past a Portuguese travel agency and a sporting goods store, I slow down to admire a row of beautiful poinsettia plants in the window of an Ecuadorian restaurant, their red flowers glowing in the sunlight. They really are perfect plants for Christmas, I think to myself. In fact, in their native Central America they're called *Flores de Noche Buena*, "Christmas Eve Flowers."

Turning to continue on my way, I start remembering the beautiful Mexican legend about the first poinsettia plants. Once there were two little children, Pepita and her cousin, Pedro. Like all children they loved the Christmas parades and parties in the days leading up to Christmas, but, being poor, they never had money to buy presents. They especially wished that they  could have something to bring to the Baby Jesus in the large manger scene inside the village church.

One Christmas Eve, the two poor children set out for church empty handed as usual, to watch as many of the other children brought their fine gifts to the Christ Child in his manger. As they got close to church, however, little Pepita grew desperate because she had no gift, and, kneeling down by the side of the road, she picked a handful of scraggly weeds, which she made into a bouquet. She was ashamed of her gift as she entered the little village chapel, but Pedro tried to comfort his cousin by saying, "You know, Pepita, that even the most humble gift, if you give it out of love, will be acceptable in his eyes."

In the midst of this reflection, my gaze drifts to a patch of weeds to my left between the curb and the sidewalk.

Of course Pepita was teased by other children when they saw her pathetic gift. But she kept silent, knowing that this was the best she could do. As she walked toward the altar where the manger scene was set up, she remembered Pedro's kind words: "You know, Pepita, that even the most humble gift, if you give it out of love, will be acceptable in his eyes." Then she knelt and carefully laid her little bouquet of plain weeds on the straw in the nativity scene as her gift to Baby Jesus.

Suddenly, in full view of everyone in the church, the green top leaves of her weeds burst into star-shaped flowers of brilliant red, and soon the whole manger was surrounded by the same beautiful crimson stars. From that day on, the deep red flowers would bloom each year during the Christmas season and would come to be known as *Flores de Noche Buena*, "Christmas Eve Flowers."

I start looking for more poinsettias in stores along the avenue. Noticing a couple of them in the window of the Mexican restaurant, I look more closely through the plate glass and see that there is a little plant on every table. Pepita's beautiful poinsettias are good reminders that God can do beautiful things with the poorest of gifts. Sometimes, for example, we show up at prayer with nothing to offer but a fistful of weeds—we may be distracted or upset or too tired to concentrate on our prayer, but the Lord, who sees our hearts, transforms our pitiful attempts at praying into a beautiful gift pleasing in God's eyes.

Walking on, I notice a patch of scraggly green weeds around the base of a tree along the sidewalk, and think about how I need to get better at spotting poinsettias when dealing with people. Maybe a grumpy response to me is the best that a person can manage on a certain morning, and maybe even that took a lot of effort on their part. Maybe a poorly done homework assignment is actually a remarkable accomplishment for a student given the horrendous circumstances he's living in at home. I pray that instead of criticizing the "weeds" that people sometimes offer me, I might be able to recognize them as gifts—like Pepita's star-shaped flowers.

Spotting another poinsettia plant in another window, a large one with white leaves instead of red ones, I begin to wonder if perhaps some of my own offerings of weeds have not turned into poinsettias now and then. A simple two-minute phone call was the best I could manage that day, but the person receiving it may have seen it as a beautiful gift of kindness and caring. Or I stand helplessly beside another person's hospital bed and smile and apologize, "I wish there were something I could do!" The sick person answers, "You've already done it!" Somehow the Lord has turned my frustrating inability to be of help into a lovely gift, my fistful of weeds has just blossomed into *flores de Noche Buena*.

I come to a busy corner by the Portuguese gift store. There are no poinsettias in view. But I look down at my feet. Sure enough, in the cracks of the sidewalk along the curb, are plenty of weeds.

Reflection

Pepita found out what God can do with a gift that is offered with love. Think of someone whose sincere efforts may not live up to your expectations; do you perhaps need to see those efforts the way God sees your own—as something not only acceptable but beautiful? Perhaps one day the sight of a poinsettia plant may encourage you not to give up, even when your efforts seem inadequate or the results disappointing.

Sacred Scripture

Now standing there were six stone water jars for the Jewish rites of purification, each holding twenty or thirty gallons. Jesus said to them, "Fill the jars with water." And they filled them up to the brim. He said to them, "Now draw some out, and take it to the chief steward." So they took it. . . . The steward tasted the water that had become wine, and did not know where it came from (though the servants who had drawn the water knew). (John 2:6–9)

Rule of Benedict

And finally, never lose hope in God's mercy. (Chapter 4, "The Tools for Good Works," v. 74)

DECEMBER 18
Homecoming Party

I step through the door from the hallway into our school's cafeteria and am immediately engulfed by waves of loud conversation and boisterous laughing. This is the annual "recent grads'" reunion, when alumni from the past several years, most of them still in college, come back to check in with old friends and see how the school is doing.

Several of last year's graduates stand in a loose circle with paper plates of hot wings and ziti, busily trading stories of their first semester in college, while a couple of older alumni in business suits are talking about their new jobs.

There is a Christmas feeling in the room, thanks in part to dozens of poinsettia plants placed on the tables. The return of the young alumni on Christmas break is one of my favorite parts of the season at Newark Abbey. For most people, the holidays offer the opportunity to get connected again with family and friends through visits, dinners, and parties like this one.

I step into the room, scanning the faces. All of them are familiar, of course, although every now and then I have to sneak a look at someone's name tag. Suddenly I'm being crushed in a rough bear hug from behind accompanied by a "Guess who!"

Luckily I come up with the right name before any ribs get crushed: "Randy! Quit trying to kill me!" Released from the heavy arms I turn around and look into the face of one of those students who make it all worthwhile. He struggled all through high school—with his books and his teachers, with his home problems and his personal demons.

As we hug each other he asks, "How you doin', Father Al?" We immediately start trading memories, including a couple of war stories from sophomore religion class. His big smile and clear eyes, and his enthusiasm for his college courses, all make me think that maybe, in the end, he may actually make it.

Another familiar voice breaks in on our conversation, this one from a fellow in a business suit, whom I recognize from several years ago. He announces that he graduated last June from his Ivy League college and is currently working for a large investment banking corporation in the suburbs. It wasn't so long ago that he was a skinny freshman finding his way timidly through the hallways here, and now he's back, making it a point to stay in touch with the place that has had such an influence on him.

It occurs to me that the bonds of love at this reunion foreshadow the coming kingdom that is foretold in the Advent readings. Staying connected with others is, in any case, an important Benedictine trait. Saint Benedict places a high value on community members' staying connected to one another, and so arranges for dozens of practices to ensure that this happens. First there are the obvious ones, such as common ownership of goods, the sharing of meals, and common liturgical prayer. But there are many more. Benedict wants the monk to ask the abbot for simple permissions, not just as a test of humility but as a way for each member to stay connected with the community. This is also why he encourages the monk to reveal his inmost thoughts to the abbot (RB 7:44) and why he wants the abbot to send a couple of wise elders to comfort any brother who seems to be getting discouraged (RB 27:2–3). He wants the monks to take turns waiting on one another at meals (RB 35:1–3) and to take special care of the sick (RB 36:1), the elderly, and the very young members of the community (RB 37:1–3). One of the severest penalties the abbot can impose on a monk is to exclude him from sharing meals with the community.

It occurs to me as I watch Randy turn to greet some friends, that Western culture emphasizes being an individual, self-sufficient and independent. Parents try to give each of their children a private bedroom, and we each listen to our own music on our headphones.

But a Latin phrase from the *Rule of Benedict* comes to mind, "*omnes pariter*," which means "all together." This is a good summary of Benedict's ideal of interconnectedness. He uses it when he asks that at the end of the psalm everyone rise "all together" to honor the Holy Trinity (RB 20:5) or that the community pray together with a newly arrived guest (RB 23:4). It is also the way the monks are to keep Lent, not as individuals but "all together" as a community (RB 49:2), and most important of all, it is the way we will arrive at our final reward, not as individuals but as a community: "Let them prefer nothing whatever to Christ, and may he bring us all together to everlasting life" (RB 72:11).

Just as our holiday get-togethers celebrate the mystery of interconnectedness, Advent and Christmas celebrate the connections which Jesus establishes: by his birth at Bethlehem he joins heaven to earth, and by taking on human flesh he connects all human beings as his brothers and sisters, children of the same heavenly Father. Our parties offer us a glimpse of that unity for which we keep praying when we sing that verse of "O Come, Emmanuel" during Advent:

> O come, Desire of nations, bind
> In one the hearts of all mankind;
> Bid thou our sad divisions cease,
> And be thyself our King of Peace.

Noticing a group of last year's graduates at the other end of the room, I head across to join them.

Reflection

Picture yourself traveling the road to heaven. Assuming that you are not on the road alone, how important is the presence of others? Do they help you to achieve your heavenly goal? Think of something you might do during Advent or Christmas to celebrate or strengthen your connection with certain people who are important to you.

Sacred Scripture

For just as the body is one and has many members, and all the members of the body, though many, are one body, so it is with Christ. For in the one Spirit we were all baptized into one body— Jews or Greeks, slaves or free—and we were all made to drink of one Spirit. Indeed, the body does not consist of one member but of many. (1 Cor. 12:12–14)

Rule of Benedict

Just as there is a wicked zeal of bitterness which separates from God and leads to hell, so there is good zeal which separates from evil and leads to God and everlasting life. This, then, is the good zeal which monks must foster with fervent love: They should each try to be the first to show respect to the other, supporting with the greatest patience one another's weaknesses of body or behavior, and earnestly competing in obedience to one another. . . . Let them prefer nothing whatever to Christ, and may he bring us all together to everlasting life. (Chapter 72, "The Good Zeal of Monks," vv. 1–6, 11–12)

December 19
Holiday Cooking

The sidewalk on Ferry Street in the Portuguese and Spanish neighborhood seems extra busy this afternoon. I pause for a moment, as I usually do, in front of the fish market to peer through the big window. Piled on trays of crushed ice are little silvery sardines, next to them lies a huge fish with shimmering orange showing under its gill slits, and, finally, there is a tangle of charcoal gray squid filling a Styrofoam container. I picture the hectic scene next week on Christmas Eve, when dozens of men and women will be standing three-deep at the long counter to buy the several kinds of fish they need for that night's traditional dinner.

As I continue my stroll, I start to think how important food is for celebrating the holidays, especially when it comes to ethnic dishes and family traditions. I remember a Thanksgiving many years ago when my mother tried a different recipe for the turkey stuffing. The unexpected break with tradition caused such consternation around the dinner table that the following year she went back to making it the "right" way.

I pass a little grocery store and peek inside, where more shoppers are crowding the narrow aisles, presumably buying ingredients for some favorite holiday dishes. As I spy on the shoppers, I ask myself what makes special holiday foods taste so good. Maybe it's because we don't get to eat them at any other time of the year, or because we associate them with the happy memories of childhood. Or maybe it's simply that they're often so loaded with butter, sugar, fat, and other great-tasting things!

I stop in front of a pastry shop to peer in at the display cases crammed with neat rows of desserts. There are golden yellow custard cupcakes, buns dusted with powdered sugar, chocolate layer cakes, and a dozen other kinds of frosted and glazed things. I decide that I had better keep walking up Ferry Street before I make myself any hungrier. Just as I'm turning to go, I notice, in the case nearest the door, cellophane-wrapped plates of Christmas cookies. As I stride away, trying to work off all those imaginary calories I just took in, it suddenly occurs to me that store-bought Christmas cookies never quite taste as good as homemade ones. Aha! Now that's interesting! Maybe the biggest reason holiday food tastes so good is because someone has painstakingly prepared it with a lot of time, work, and loving care.

And "loving care" is actually a very biblical idea. In the Old Testament it refers to God's consistent, ever-faithful, relentless, lavish, and unrestrained love for Israel. In the New Testament it refers to the boundless, unconditional love that Jesus showed throughout his life, and which he calls us to imitate. Saint Paul calls this kind of love *agapē*, the greatest of gifts: "Love is patient; love is kind; love is not envious or boastful or arrogant or rude. It does not insist on its own way" (1 Cor. 13:4–5). *Agapē* is what lies behind the whole Christmas event, "For God so loved the world that he gave his only Son" (John 3:16).

I notice my reflection glide across the plate glass window of the gift shop. On a shelf there is a beautiful platter decorated with a bright hand-painted cornucopia spilling forth yellow squash, orange pumpkins, green corncobs, clusters of purple grapes, a couple of red apples, and a golden pear. In this area of town, which has always boasted a variety of ethnic neighborhoods, a big platter like this on a Christmas dinner table could hold any one of a number of different treats. In a Portuguese or an Italian family it might be used for the fish on Christmas Eve. In a German family it might be piled with pastries and cookies—*Lebkuchen*, *Pfeffernüsse*, and *Springerle*. A Central or South American cook might use it to serve golden, sugar-dusted fritters called *buñuelos*.

All those homemade holiday pastries and foods, prepared with such hard work and loving care, are reflections of God's own selfless love and signs that the kingdom is already among us in our homes and families.

Since the early monastic tradition saw the monastery as a reflection of the heavenly kingdom, it's not surprising that Benedict is always encouraging his monks to look outside of themselves and toward others in loving concern—a love that is undeserved and unmerited. In a world of reciprocity, of "you scratch my back and I'll scratch yours," such love breaks the cycle of payback and reaches a person as a true gift, one that comes without strings attached. This is precisely the kind of love God showed to us on that first Christmas.

As we prepare to celebrate God's selfless gift of love in the babe at Bethlehem, our holiday cooking, often done with so much tender loving care, is a wonderful parable of that same kind of gift, because it too comes from love that is freely given with no expectation of return.

I continue walking toward the railroad station and, a mile away, the monastery. There are no more food stores between here and home, but I have more than enough delightful images to reflect on: not just mouthwatering holiday dishes, but the love that so often creates them and that is, after all, what the holy days are all about.

Reflection

Think of someone you know who seems to enjoy cooking for people as a way of loving family and friends, with no expectation of return. Do you ever have opportunities to love without expecting anything in return? Think of how you might use some such opportunity during the season of Advent or Christmas.

Sacred Scripture

For this reason I bow my knees before the Father, from whom every family in heaven and on earth takes its name. I pray that, according to the riches of his glory, he may grant that you may be strengthened in your inner being with power through his Spirit, and that Christ may dwell in your hearts through faith, as you are being rooted and grounded in love. I pray that you may have the power to comprehend, with all the saints, what is the breadth and length and height and depth, and to know the love of Christ that surpasses knowledge, so that you may be filled with all the fullness of God. (Eph. 3:14–19)

Rule of Benedict

No one is to pursue what he judges better for himself, but instead, what he judges better for someone else. To their fellow monks they show the pure love of brothers; to God, loving fear; to their abbot, unfeigned and humble love. (Chapter 72, "The Good Zeal of Monks," vv. 7–10)

DECEMBER 20

Vacation Time

A s I stand at the street corner in front of the abbey church waiting for the light to change, I look up the hill towards Saint Mary's Elementary School. There seems to be a lot of activity up there—cars with flashers on, and traffic slowing to a crawl. When I see a woman scurrying across the street holding a little boy by the hand, I remember that this is the last day of school at Saint Mary's and the start of Christmas vacation. The scene looks so interesting that I decide to cross King Boulevard and walk up for a closer look.

Now I can hear the excited shrieks of some children in the play yard and see some first-graders wearing miniature backpacks crossing William Street with their parents to climb into waiting cars. There is a mood of exuberance and celebration. Watching them, it occurs to me that children are probably much better than we grownups at spending their leisure time aimlessly and enjoying the sudden freedom from their usual routine.

As I walk past the children piling into parked cars, I start thinking about the word "vacation." It comes from the Latin verb *vacare*, "to be free for, to have leisure for." I remember it used to come up during our common prayer in the days when we prayed the Psalms in Latin: "*Vacate et videte quoniam ego sum Deus*" (Ps. 46:10), which we now translate as "Be still, and know that I am God." "*Vacate*, be still" is not easy for me to put into practice. It took me some years to learn how to relax and savor each hour of a school vacation, and I'm still learning how to be still and savor the periods assigned each day in the monastic schedule for quiet prayer and reading.

It's interesting that Saint Benedict uses *vacare* when he schedules times for the monks' holy reading: "Let them devote themselves to [*vacare*, be free for, have leisure for] their holy reading" (RB 48:4). For this "holy leisure," he assigns several of the best hours of each day, when the monks will be fully awake and at their best. Such time spent without pressure, without external activity, and without discernible results is an integral part of the balanced life that he envisions.

I find it hard to sit still and simply *be* with God because I'm not accomplishing anything useful and have no results to show. Rather than being "on vacation for God" I prefer rolling up my sleeves and doing things. There is this tug of war in my heart between Martha working in the kitchen and Mary sitting quietly at the Lord's feet (Luke 10:38–42), between the desire to do things and the need to see the deeper meaning of the things that I'm doing.

An early Christian spiritual writer once observed that Martha and Mary have to learn to live together as sisters under the same roof. No matter what my vocation, or how many my obligations, I cannot simply let Martha dictate my life. Once I leave her alone in the kitchen, she always loses her sense of what's important, and her work, which could theoretically bring her closer to God, becomes a burden that makes her frustrated, angry, and envious of Mary.

As I watch these busy parents picking up their children, I start to think that while productive activity and good works are important, they are not enough for a Christian; we have to be people of prayer first and devote at least some time to "*vacare Deo.*" It occurs to me that the first meaning of *vacare* is "to be empty"; we need, then, to make some empty space for God in our busy lives. This "empty" time allows us to stop, put aside all our worries, and just love the Lord our God with our whole heart, our whole soul, and our whole strength. This may be the hardest part of being a Christian in the twenty-first century: trying to find a few moments each day to forget the constant pressure to achieve and to turn all our attention instead to the one thing that really matters in the end, to simply be with the One who is the author of all being.

I've passed the school and the excitement on the sidewalk. As I get to the end of William Street, I turn around and head back the way I came. On my left, I notice our high school's residence hall, reminding me that our own Christmas break starts tomorrow. I pray that I'll be able to use this vacation as an opportunity to *vacare*, to stop being so productive, and to spend a lot of quiet time being still and paying attention to God—which is, after all, what I hope to be doing for all eternity in heaven.

As I keep heading back down the hill, I glance at my watch. I want to be back in the monastery by four o'clock, so that I'll have an hour before mass for my daily afternoon "vacation time" with the Lord.

Reflection

Is there a specific area in which your "Martha" side tends to take over and cause you to lose perspective on what is most important in Christian life? Is there something you might do to help yourself achieve more balance between the practical, active side of your life and the reflective, listening side, especially during this busy time of the year? Pray that Martha and Mary will learn to live in harmony as sisters in your heart.

Sacred Scripture

The apostles gathered around Jesus, and told him all that they had done and taught. He said to them, "Come away to a deserted place all by yourselves and rest a while." For many were coming and going, and they had no leisure even to eat. And they went away in the boat to a deserted place by themselves. (Mark 6:30–32)

Rule of Benedict

On hearing the signal for an hour of the divine office, the monk will immediately set aside what he has in hand and go with utmost speed. . . . Indeed, nothing is to be preferred to the Work of God. (Chapter 43, "Tardiness at the Work of God or at Table," vv. 1, 3)

DECEMBER 21

Putting Up Lights

I've walked across the bridge into Harrison, an old industrial suburb of Newark on the other side of the Passaic River. I turn down Sussex Street, lined by brick row houses on both sides, and I head down the long block with the late afternoon sun at my back. As I walk along I can't help noticing how dreary the street seems. In August there are beds of bright flowers along the driveways and front walks, but now in December all the flowers are gone, and the lawns are a dusty tan.

As I make my way farther through the lengthening shadows, though, I notice that the dreariness will not remain for long. Several of the little front lawns seem to have sprouted big plastic candles and life-size wooden Santa cutouts with spotlights pointed at them. Lots of the evergreen shrubs are covered with miniature glass bulbs that will come to life this evening; electric candles sit on inside windowsills. During the long, dark winter nights, there is something encouraging and life-giving about all those candles and glimmering electric bulbs. In an hour this whole street will be glowing with Christmas, even though it hasn't arrived yet.

These lights, it suddenly occurs to me, turn a walk down Sussex Street into a powerful parable about Advent and of all of Christian life. Matthew reminds us of Isaiah's prophesy, "The people who walked in darkness have seen a great light; those who dwelt in a land of deep darkness, on them has light shined" (Isa. 9:2, cited in Matt. 4:16). Jesus proclaims, "I am the light of the world; he who follows me will not walk in darkness, but will have the light of life" (John 8:12).

The sun is dropping fast now, and will soon set behind the buildings along the downtown Newark skyline. I think of Benedict's warning from John's gospel, "Run while you have the light of life, that the darkness of death may not overtake you [John 12:35]." As I start walking faster, I think about how John reminds all Christians that we are called to walk in the light of Christ: "If we walk in the light, as he is in the light, we have fellowship with one another, and the blood of Jesus his Son cleanses us from all sin" (1 John 1:7).

Perhaps the most striking and challenging image of light comes in the Sermon on the Mount, when our Lord declares, "You are the light of the world. . . . your light must shine before others, that they may see your good deeds and glorify your heavenly Father" (Matt. 5:14, 16). I wonder if I am much of a light for my students in class, or for my brother monks who live with me. Saint Benedict seems to envision a community in which each member is a light for the others. Sometimes as we light the candles in our community's Advent wreath in the refectory at supper, I imagine that there are not four candles but seventeen—one for each monk in our community. Each imaginary candle offers its light to the others, contributing to the brightness of the whole, and together we light the entire room, so that people passing by on the sidewalk can see the glow.

I walk past a little neighborhood tavern with its weatherworn sign in Portuguese. I glance into the dark interior and see more lights—tiny white ones that outline the big mirror behind the bar. Then I turn down Warren Street. Among the big, bleak factory buildings, a few little houses make a brave show with strands of Christmas lights along the outside edges of their windows. I notice that, up ahead on Rodgers Boulevard, waves of commuters returning from Manhattan have already started pouring out of the train station. The December dusk is deepening. I keep up my pace, hoping to get home before dark, cheered by Harrison's holiday lights and remembering the task that we have each been given at our Baptism, to be the light of the world.

Reflection

As you put up lights as holiday decorations or see them in various places this Advent, ask yourself how you might be more of a light to those around you, especially in your home and your workplace.

Meditate on the verses from the prologue to John's gospel that follow, in which the word *light* appears seven times.

Sacred Scripture

What has come into being in him was life, and the life was the light of all people. The light shines in the darkness, and the darkness did not overcome it. There was a man sent from God, whose name was John. He came as a witness to testify to the light, so that all might believe through him. He himself was not the light, but he came to testify to the light. The true light, which enlightens everyone, was coming into the world. (John 1:3b–9)

Wisdom of the Desert

Abba Lot went to see Abba Joseph and said to him: Abba, as much as I am able I practice a small rule, a little fasting, some prayer and meditation, and remain quiet and as much as possible I keep my thoughts clean. What else should I do? Then the old man stood up and stretched his hands toward heaven, and his fingers became like ten torches of flame and he said to him: If you wish, you can become all flame.[22]

---

22. Gregory Mayers, *Listen to the Desert* (Liguori, MO: Triumph Books, 1996), 54.

DECEMBER 22
Holiday Hospitality

I'm walking along Elm Street in the Ironbound, past neat narrow wooden houses that push right up to the sidewalk. Their windows often sport Brazilian or Portuguese flags, and now and then a set of six blue and white tiles on the front of the house will depict Our Lady of Fatima and the three children to whom she appeared. A smoky barbecue aroma wafts from the corner *churrasquiera*, making me think about lunch.

In the middle of the block, up ahead, a young man opens the back door of an SUV parked at the curb and leans in to get something. As he backs out and straightens up, he is carrying a deep cooking tray covered with aluminum foil. On top of this is a large plastic bowl covered with a lid. A young woman has gotten out of the front seat on the passenger side and has come around to supervise the operation while holding a sleepy-looking baby bundled in a pale blue snowsuit.

Even before Christmas, the holy days of Advent are a time for welcoming relatives and friends into our homes for holiday parties, visits, and special meals. In fact, it is at this time of year, more than at any other, that we come to appreciate something of the Bible's sense of the sacredness of hospitality, of welcoming others into our homes. The book of Genesis shows Abraham offering lavish hospitality to three perfect strangers who, it turns out, are divine messengers (Gen. 18:1–15). The author of Hebrews recalls this story when he advises his readers, "Do not neglect to show hospitality to strangers, for by doing that some have entertained angels without knowing it" (Heb. 13:2). Saint Benedict continues the tradition, making hospitality a central monastic virtue. He begins his chapter on the reception of guests with the instruction, "All guests who present themselves are to be welcomed as Christ" (RB 53:1).

As I approach the young family, the woman with the baby turns and waves at someone. I follow her gaze and see, standing at the top of the steep front steps of a nearby house, a thin, middle-aged woman. Framed in the doorway, she returns the wave and calls out a greeting that I can't quite hear. Behind her the door stands wide open in welcome.

The early church added a new dimension to the sacredness of hospitality with the phrase "in the Lord." Paul writes to the Christians in Rome, for instance, "I commend to you our sister Phoebe, a deaconess of the church at Cenchreae, that you may receive her in the Lord" (Rom. 16:1–2). He asks a similar favor of the Philippians on behalf of his friend Epaphroditus: "So receive him in the Lord with all joy" (Phil. 2:29).

Christians, then, are to receive one another "in the Lord." Benedict carries on that tradition when he calls for his monks to receive all guests as if they were Christ himself (RB 53:1). And so, as we welcome our Christmas guests "in the Lord," it's a great reminder that we are also about to welcome the newborn Savior into our homes.

By now I'm passing the house just as the front door closes behind the guests. I wonder if that grandmother realizes that she is carrying on a long and sacred biblical tradition.

The New Testament verb "to welcome, to receive" also came to mean "to await, to look forward expectantly," not unlike this grandmother as she was waiting for the young couple to arrive with her grandson. The Advent scriptures are filled with images of people waiting for someone to arrive. "Let your loins be girded and your lamps burning, and be like men who are waiting for their master to come home from the marriage feast, so that they may open to him at once when he comes and knocks" (Luke 12:25–36). At the time of the presentation of the child Jesus in the temple, there were two holy people there to welcome Jesus. First was the aged Simeon, who is "righteous and devout, looking for ["awaiting"] the consolation of Israel, and the Holy Spirit was upon him" (Luke 2:25). The second was an elderly woman: "And coming up at that very hour [Anna] gave thanks to God, and spoke of him to all who were looking for ["awaiting"] the redemption of Jerusalem" (Luke 2:28).

As I continue down the street, it seems to me that I can almost feel people in their houses waiting expectantly for their guests to arrive, waiting to receive them "in the Lord." I hope that they sense somehow that they are echoing the church's longing for the arrival of our Savior. Receiving visitors is a foretaste of the day when we will welcome Christ, for whom we wait with longing and to whom we have been praying all during Advent, "Maranatha! Come, Lord Jesus!"

Reflection

Think of people you are expecting to welcome as guests—and who, Benedict tells us, should be received as Christ. Are some of them easier to welcome than others? Who are the guests in whom you find it easiest to see Christ? Are there some in whom you find it difficult to experience the presence of Christ? You might pray that you will be able to see and welcome Christ in each one of them.

Sacred Scripture

The Lord appeared to Abraham by the oaks of Mamre, as he sat at the entrance of his tent in the heat of the day. He looked up and saw three men standing near him. When he saw them, he ran from the tent entrance to meet them, and bowed down to the ground. He said, "My lord, if I find favor with you, do not pass by your servant. Let a little water be brought, and wash your feet, and rest yourselves under the tree. Let me bring a little bread, that you may refresh yourselves, and after that you may pass on—since you have come to your servant." So they said, "Do as you have said." And Abraham hastened into the tent to Sarah, and said, "Make ready quickly three measures of choice flour, knead it, and make cakes." Abraham ran to the herd, and took a calf, tender and good, and gave it to the servant, who hastened to prepare it. Then he took curds and milk and the calf that he had prepared, and set it before them; and he stood by them under the tree while they ate. (Gen. 18:1–8)

Wisdom of the Desert

A brother came and stayed with a certain solitary and when he was leaving he said: Forgive me, Father, for I have broken in upon your Rule. But the hermit replied, saying: My Rule is to receive you with hospitality and to let you go in peace.[23]

---

23. Thomas Merton, *The Wisdom of the Desert* (New York: New Directions, 1970), 51.

DECEMBER 23
Visiting

I step carefully down the steep front stairs to the sidewalk on Walnut Street. They're familiar now, after almost twenty years of visiting the Pontevedra family. I taught all three of the sons in school and have remained friends with the family, walking down here once or twice a year for Sunday dinner. But today's was just an impromptu visit, the result of meeting Mrs. Pontevedra on the sidewalk as she was getting out of her car. She invited me up for coffee and some Spanish pastries. That was more than an hour ago.

At the bottom of the steps I turn and start the twenty-five-minute walk home, happy for the pleasant and unexpected visit. I start to think how the holidays give us the opportunity to do a lot of visiting, sometimes with relatives or friends that we don't see at any other time of year. In any case, planned or otherwise, visiting is an important part of the holidays. It is also, as I recall, a rich biblical image full of meaning for both Advent and Christmas.

The Old Testament speaks of God as actively involved in the history of the Israelites, as "visiting" various individuals. But, when the Lord of History "visits," the verb[24] has the dual sense of "visit" and "be concerned about." For instance, the Lord "visits" Sarah and she bears a son, Isaac (Gen. 21:1). The patriarch Joseph promises his brothers that God will surely "visit" them and lead them out of Egypt (Gen. 50:24). And God promises the Jews in exile, "I myself will look after and tend ["visit"] my sheep" (Ezek. 34:11 NAB).

---

24. Greek *episkeptomai*.

Still walking up Walnut Street, I notice that there are no empty parking places along the curb, which is unusual for mid-afternoon. Maybe there are more Christmas visitors in the neighborhood than just me.

The image of God's visiting the world carries over from the Old Testament into the New. When Zachary, the father of John the Baptist, is filled with gratitude at the birth of his son, he sings the beautiful Canticle of Zachary, the *Benedictus* (Luke 1:68–79), a hymn in praise of this God who visits. It begins "Blessed be the Lord, the God of Israel, for he has visited and brought redemption to his people" (Luke 1:68 NAB). Here "visited" and "brought redemption" both mean the same thing. Then near the end of his song Zachary prays, "because of the tender mercy of our God by which the daybreak from on high will visit us" (v. 78 NAB). In this canticle, God is decidedly not a guest dropping by for a quick hello; the Lord's visit has a clear purpose: to bring us healing and salvation.

I turn right on to Jefferson Street and see, up ahead, some visitors walking up the front steps of Saint James Hospital, carrying plastic bags and a couple of helium-filled balloons. It occurs to me that Jesus expects us to imitate this loving Lord who is constantly visiting us to heal and help us; He demands that we do the same for others. In fact, Jesus promises that ultimately, our entrance into the kingdom will be decided on the basis of how well we have imitated the God who "visits": "Come, you who are blessed by my Father.... For I was ... sick and you visited me" (Matt. 25:34, 36 NJB). Our Savior is not talking about occasional, casual acts of kindness, but rather about a fundamental attitude toward others. We need to become "visitors," to be God's healing hand, God's consoling voice, God's calming presence in the midst of the world's chaotic clamor.

As I get closer to the hospital, I start to look at my own "visits," my interactions with others. Are my encounters with my brother monks as life-giving as God's visit to Sarah? Are my interactions with my friends as up-building and encouraging as Jesus' visits to Martha, Mary, and Lazarus? This holy season challenges me to spend not just Advent and Christmas but every day of my life imitating the God who "visits" us, by bringing God's love and healing to my brothers and sisters.

Continuing homeward in the light of the weak winter sun, I turn left at the corner. Lafayette Street stretches ahead of me for blocks, but there's not a free parking place to be seen. More Christmas visitors in the neighborhood, no doubt.

Reflection

Think of some visits you have made during the holidays (or perhaps some that are still to come), and reflect on each of them in terms of the wider biblical sense of "visit."

When do your encounters with others tend to be life-giving and healing for you or for the other person? When do they sometimes fall short?

Sacred Scripture

As he drew near to the gate of the city, a man who had died was being carried out, the only son of his mother, and she was a widow. A large crowd from the city was with her. When the Lord saw her, he was moved with pity for her and said to her, "Do not weep." He stepped forward and touched the coffin; at this the bearers halted, and he said, "Young man, I tell you, arise!" The dead man sat up and began to speak, and Jesus gave him to his mother. Fear seized them all, and they glorified God, exclaiming, "A great prophet has arisen in our midst," and "God has visited his people." (Luke 7:12–16 NAB)

Rule of Benedict

[A monk visiting from another monastery] may, indeed, with all humility and love make some reasonable criticisms or observations, which the abbot should prudently consider; it is possible that the Lord guided him to the monastery for this very purpose. (Chapter 61, "The Reception of Visiting Monks," v. 4)

December 24

Some Assembly Required

The wide sidewalk on Broad Street across from Military Park is thick with shoppers bustling between the several stores on the block. These are the real last-minute shoppers, I figure, since this is the afternoon of Christmas Eve. As I stroll along, I start to think about my own preparations in the monastery, which have all been taken care of: all the music is set for 5:00 p.m. First Vespers of the Nativity, as well as for the Christmas vigil and midnight mass. I've put up the garlands in the refectory around the icon and in the big chandelier.

I slow down to make way for a man coming out of a discount store carrying a box about four feet long. Judging from the way he's holding it, it must be pretty heavy. On its front panel is a large full-color picture of a little girl kneeling in front of a three-foot high plastic doll house with a pink roof and blue trim. Above the picture, big blue block letters announce PLASTIC DOLL HOUSE. Once out on the sidewalk, the man stops to adjust his grip on the unwieldy carton, and as I walk by I notice, printed in smaller block letters at the bottom of the picture, the obvious but ominous phrase ASSEMBLY REQUIRED.

I smile and say to myself, "Well, good luck, Buddy." I've had enough experience putting together factory-made items that I can imagine the ordeal this fellow may be in for. A cousin of mine was up all night one Christmas Eve struggling to put together some sort of slot-racing track for one of his children. He got finished just as the sun started coming up, in time to preserve Santa's good name—but he spent Christmas day in a tired stupor.

99

As I get to the other side of the wide boulevard, it occurs to me that life is something like that: God gives us all the pieces we need and then expects us to make something beautiful out of them. We have to fashion our lives from our talents and predispositions, our experiences and our physical abilities or disabilities, and our personality traits. We don't get a diagram or directions to work from, either; we have to wing it. We get some general guidelines such as "Do everything out of love" and "Let peace be your aim," but for the most part we're not quite sure how the details are supposed to work.

I pass in front of another discount store and notice the big boxes stacked high against the plate glass window: molded plastic castles, haunted houses, and Barbie palaces, each undoubtedly bearing the same little notice: ASSEMBLY REQUIRED. Leaving the window behind me I start wondering why God can't just hand me my life ready made: no assembly needed, no wondering, no guesswork.

Then I think of the nativity scene in the back of our church. Jesus, Mary, and Joseph each had to do a lot of work to make sense of the events in their lives. Poor Saint Joseph had to deal with dreams telling him to take Mary as his spouse, and angels and mysterious voices ordering him to take his family and flee into Egypt or to return to Israel. I wonder how long it took him to figure out what was going on. Some assembly was definitely required in his life!

Mary, too, had to put things together as best she could—the message from Gabriel, her miraculous pregnancy, the mysterious visitors and messages surrounding her baby's birth. Luke says that "she kept pondering all these things in her heart" (Luke 2:19, 51). And she was still pondering thirty years later, trying to fit things together at the foot of the cross.

And what about baby Jesus lying there in the manger? In recent years, theologians have been reminding us that, if Jesus is fully human, he cannot have been born with a fully developed self-consciousness and a clear sense of his life's mission. He would have had to grow in self-knowledge just like the rest of us and put things together as he went. "Jesus increased in wisdom and in years," according to Luke 2:52, and his baptism in the Jordan and his temptations in the desert were important times of self-discovery for the young Messiah.

Even in the gospel of John, in which Jesus is so often portrayed as all knowing and in complete control, there is an intriguing verse that seems to show Jesus putting things together little by little. In the third chapter of John, Jesus seems to be using a process of trial and error, experimenting with a ministry of baptism for a short time; perhaps wondering if he was supposed to imitate his cousin John the Baptist. The gospel writer tells us simply, "After this Jesus and his disciples went into the Judean countryside, and he spent some time there with them and baptized" (John 3:32). This verse should be a comfort to anyone who has ever wondered what God is up to in his or her life or has had to make a difficult decision without knowing if it was really the right one. Maybe we ought to have a painting of Jesus baptizing in the Jordan, experimenting and trying to find out what ministry he was being called to.

I check my watch and, seeing that it's after three, decide to pick up my pace so I can be back at the monastery with some time left before mass to read my Bible, maybe Luke's account of the birth in Bethlehem.

As I turn up Commerce Street in the direction of the monastery, I reflect on Jesus, Mary, and Joseph in the stable at Bethlehem. Each of them is a model of faithfulness, of how to live in faith while trying to figure things out, when it is not at all clear what God wants. Their lives were like yours and mine, and like that plastic dollhouse: the pieces are all there, but assembly is required.

Reflection

Have you ever experienced having to make a significant decision about your life without being sure that it was the correct one? Think of some important question or decision facing you, and ask Jesus to give you the grace to put all the pieces together correctly.

Reflect on the verse cited in the scripture section immediately below. Try to imagine what Jesus is feeling and thinking as he baptizes people in the Jordan, imitating his cousin, John the Baptist, who is baptizing a few miles away. What questions might Jesus be asking himself? What is he asking of his heavenly Father?

Sacred Scripture

After this, Jesus and his disciples went into the region of Judea, where he spent some time with them baptizing. (John 3:22)

Wisdom of the Desert

An elder said: The reason why we do not get anywhere is that we do not know our limits, and we are not patient in carrying on the work we have begun. But without any labor at all we want to gain possession of virtue.[25]

---

25. Thomas Merton, *The Wisdom of the Desert* (New York: New Directions, 1970), 51.

DECEMBER 25

Christmas Presents

I step out of the front door of the monastery this cold and sunny Christmas morning and pause at the top of the big, stone steps, deciding which direction to walk. I decide to head to my right, which will take me down past the outdoor nativity scene at the corner. At the bottom of the steps I turn into the icy wind and notice occasional snowflakes flashing by, but not enough of them to make a white Christmas. I set off at a slow pace so that I can take a good look at the manger scene across the street. The shepherds are there, and Mary and Joseph, and of course the baby lying on the straw.

A car is stopped at the light. Poking out from the top of a large bag on the back seat are three packages wrapped in shiny red paper and white ribbon. I start to picture the hundreds of millions of presents being given and received and opened this morning, and millions of children right now playing with new toys and games. Suddenly I'm back in my childhood home on Christmas morning: my brother, my sister, and I are waiting at the top of the stairs in our pajamas and bathrobes. Finally we're told that it's OK to come down and see what Santa has brought us. Down the stairs we race, hardly noticing the beautiful scent of pine from the tree or the Christmas music coming from the record player; we head right away for the presents lying underneath the tree.

Along with the scarves and shirts, there were always some of the things I had asked for—a model airplane kit, a slot-racing track, or some other popular toy. But most of the gifts I remember best are the ones I had never asked for. My favorite was a quiz game, which over the space of months taught me dozens of pieces of useful information, such as Thomas Edison's middle name. (I still remember it: Alva.)

Edison's light bulb—now a traffic signal—has changed to green, and as I start across Springfield Avenue I take a last glance at the manger. I notice that the three wise men aren't there yet—they won't show up with their gifts until the feast of the Epiphany, almost two weeks away. It occurs to me that many people think it was the wise men who started all of this gift-giving two thousand years ago, when they came to Bethlehem bearing gifts of gold and frankincense and myrrh (Matt. 2:11). Actually, though, the very first and most important Christmas gift was given before the wise men got there, when God gave us the Christ Child: "For God so loved the world that he gave his only Son, that whoever believes in him should not perish but have eternal life" (John 3:16). The Lord gives us not only the Christ Child, but everything else as well.

I start thinking again about all those gifts I received but had never asked for. Then I begin counting up all the gifts God has given me, and realize that most of them I never asked for at all: my family, my faith, my monastic calling, my friends, my talents for languages and music. The list of gifts flows easily, making me realize once again how good God has been to me.

I cross West Market, still adding effortlessly to my list: my health, my good education, my teaching vocation. I realize that I've barely started. The litany of God's gifts could go on for two more blocks.

A couple of cars rush along King Boulevard; I wonder if they're on their way to deliver presents from Santa Claus. I start to think that, as a monk, I don't get to give many presents at Christmas—just a few small ones for nieces and nephews. Suddenly I remember something that Pope John Paul once wrote: the deepest human drama, he said, is to make oneself into a gift. At Christmas we celebrate God's becoming a gift for us by taking on our human flesh. But Christmas is also a call to me to imitate God by making myself into a gift for others. Every time I prepare a class, write a homily, or go out of my way to help someone, I am making myself into a gift to them.

Continuing down the street, I think again about the millions of gifts being given right at this moment. Many of them, I'd like to think, ones that weren't even asked for.

Reflection

On this Christmas Day, think of the gifts that God has given you over the years. Make a list of several of them and, as you look at each one, ask yourself some questions: Did you ask for this gift? How have you shown

God that you appreciate this gift? Is God perhaps expecting you to do still more with it?

The traditional list of "the seven gifts of the Holy Spirit" is based on the passage cited in the scripture section that follows.

Sacred Scripture

A shoot shall come out from the stock of Jesse, and a branch shall grow out of his roots. The spirit of the Lord shall rest on him, the spirit of wisdom and understanding, the spirit of counsel and might, the spirit of knowledge and the fear of the Lord. His delight shall be in the fear of the Lord. (Isa. 11:1–3)

Wisdom of Saint Basil

Now if we bear a natural love and good will toward our benefactors and undergo any kind of hardship to make a return for what was first rendered to us, what words can fitly treat the gifts of God? So many are they in number as even to defy enumeration; so great and marvelous are they that a single one of them claims for the Giver all our gratitude. (*The Long Rules*, Q.2)[26]

---

26. Saint Basil, *The Long Rules-I* (Boston: St. Paul Editions, 1950), 22.

December 26

Stopping Christmas

Taking advantage of Christmas vacation, I'm on a long walk that is taking me across the Passaic River, once again through a residential neighborhood in Harrison. The chilly air is invigorating but makes me want to keep a quick pace along Sussex Street. I glance at the empty cartons that line the curb: boxes that recently held toys, computers, and coffee makers. With my head bowed slightly against the wintry wind I almost trip over a large discarded Christmas tree lying halfway across the sidewalk, a few strands of tinsel still tangled in its bare branches. It would look strange enough at the curbside anyway, but what makes it even stranger is that this is only the day after Christmas.

As I reach the corner of Rodgers Boulevard, I notice the big drug store in the strip mall right across the street and decide to go over and buy a couple of things that I need. As the light turns green and I head across toward the store, I start to wonder about people who get rid of their Christmas tree on December 26. What makes them need to put such a sudden halt to Christmas? Maybe they put up their tree weeks ago and were tired of it? Or maybe their sense of order tells them that since Christmas is over they should get rid of the Christmas decorations right away.

The church sees Christmas very differently: she is so enthralled with the feast of Christmas that she keeps celebrating it in her liturgy for a full eight days. All this week we will sing the same Christmas psalms at Vespers. This "octave of Christmas," besides prolonging the joy of the celebration, is a powerful statement that the birth of Jesus is not just a one-time event that happened two thousand years ago and was over the next day. Christians believe that the incarnation is never over; it happened back in Bethlehem, of course, but it has kept right on happening ever since.

I step through the sliding door into the drugstore. Even though I was expecting a change, I'm still shocked: Valentine's Day has completely replaced the Christmas holidays. *Already*? I muse to myself. All of the display shelves near the front are filled with heart-shaped boxes of candy, pink toys, fake flowers, balloons, and stuffed animals proclaiming, "My Valentine!" The transformation has been swift and complete: all the Santa dolls, holiday decorations, and Christmas candies have vanished in the blink of an eye, as if some evil wizard has bewitched the whole store.

Happily for us, however, whether the stores reflect it or not, the church will continue celebrating the Christmas season for another twelve days or so. And, even better, Christmas will keep happening in our lives every day of the year, as Jesus comes to us daily in each person we meet, especially in those people that Saint Benedict loves to point out: in the poor, the guest, the very young, and the sick. And, just as important, he continues to be born in each of us through every act of self-giving love, in every gesture of generosity or loving service. I start to imagine for a moment a world in which everyone actually allowed Jesus to be born in them every day, so that his hand could touch everyone who needs healing, and his words could comfort everyone who needs consoling.

On my way down an aisle, I pass a little section of Christmas items marked down for quick sale—wrapping paper, Christmas tree lights, and candy canes—and I start to think about those "Christmas stores" that are open year round, selling every conceivable Christmas item, from artificial trees to hand-carved nativity sets. Although the owners of these businesses may be unaware of it, these stores can also have the unintended but valuable effect of reminding Christians that the mystery of the incarnation is supposed to last all year long and that it is up to each of us to make sure that Christ keeps taking flesh in our world. Each of us has to live a life of love so that Christ keeps coming to dwell among us each day of the year—no matter what the stores may be displaying on their shelves.

As I continue down the aisle, leaving the Christmas items behind me, I ask the newborn Savior to continue living in every heart, in every home— and especially in that family which has already discarded its Christmas tree.

Reflection

Think of someone who has brought Christ's presence into your life through his or her love and concern for you. Can you think of people for whom you are or could be the presence of Christ?

Saint Benedict is fond of pointing out that Christ is present in the people around us—especially the least likely ones. Think of a couple of people whom you find difficult, and reflect on the fact that each of them is Christ present in your life.

Sacred Scripture

Then the king will say to those at his right hand, "Come, you that are blessed by my Father, inherit the kingdom prepared for you from the foundation of the world; for I was hungry and you gave me food, I was thirsty and you gave me something to drink, I was a stranger and you welcomed me, I was naked and you gave me clothing, I was sick and you took care of me, I was in prison and you visited me." (Matt. 25:34–36)

Rule of Benedict

All guests who present themselves are to be welcomed as Christ, for he himself will say: I was a stranger and you welcomed me. . . . All humility should be shown in addressing a guest on arrival or departure. By a bow of the head or by a complete prostration of the body, Christ is to be adored because he is indeed welcomed in them. . . . Great care and concern are to be shown in receiving poor people and pilgrims, because in them more particularly Christ is received. (Chapter 53, "The Reception of Guests," vv. 1, 6–7, 15)

DECEMBER 27
Holiday Dinner

The narrow houses on Jackson Street are crammed shoulder to shoulder, their front doors opening directly onto the pavement. A young man carrying a shopping bag stops a few yards in front of me and rings the doorbell of a house. Just as I come alongside him the door opens and I can hear the loud, happy chatter of several voices all talking at once. The sounds seem to be coming from the first floor dining room whose windows face the street. I recall visiting someone on this street and remember the cramped feeling in the combination living room and dining room of the "railroad flat."

As the door closes behind him I imagine a dozen people crowded around a long table enjoying one another's company. Holiday meals, it occurs to me, are very special gatherings. They help us moderns to appreciate why the Israelites considered eating together to be such a significant and even sacred act. The Bible tells of dozens of festive meals big and small, held by kings and queens, emperors and generals, tax collectors and Pharisees, and even Jesus himself.

But there is a lot more to Jesus' banquets than first meets the eye. He and his fellow Jews were familiar with the traditional Old Testament image of the "messianic banquet." Isaiah, for instance, describes it this way: "On this mountain the Lord of hosts will make for all peoples a feast of rich food, a feast of well-matured wines, of rich food filled with marrow, of well-matured wines strained clear" (Isa. 25:6). Jesus picks up this banquet imagery in several parables, and in his response to the faith of a gentile centurion declares, "I tell you, many will come from east and west and will eat with Abraham and Isaac and Jacob in the kingdom of heaven" (Matt. 8:11).

I continue along Jackson Street, listening for more sounds of holiday celebrations. Loud Brazilian music pours down onto the street from a second-floor window.

Jesus does not just talk about banquets, however, but makes them a central feature of his ministry. In fact, it seems that wherever Jesus goes there are banquets. These meals and their free-for-all welcome of disreputable people and social outcasts speak powerfully about his vision: a kingdom based on God's total acceptance and boundless forgiveness. So, when Jesus eats with tax collectors and sinners, he is revealing a central if unsettling truth about the kingdom of God: it will be open to everyone. A modern writer summarizes Jesus' idea this way: "The banquet of the kingdom is open to everyone who is willing to sit down with anyone." The pious Jewish leaders were not ready to sit down with just anyone.

It occurs to me that a holiday meal with lots of people around a table can speak as eloquently about the kingdom as those banquets that Jesus enjoyed. He is just as present at a joyful holiday celebration in a crowded living room on Jackson Street in Newark as he was in Zacchaeus the tax-collector's house in Jericho.

A family celebration, however, does more than just foreshadow the messianic banquet of heaven, it challenges me to look at the way I see other people. Is everyone welcome at the table of my life, or are there whole groups of people whom I exclude from my life? Is there some particular person who is no longer welcome? Am I getting in practice for the heavenly banquet by the way I treat people who are different from me or whose ideas clash with mine?

Now I'm at the corner of Ferry Street, the busy shopping area for the neighborhood. It has always been home to merchants of many nationalities: Germans, Poles, Lithuanians, Italians, and Irish and, more recently, Spanish, Portuguese, and Latin Americans. Ferry Street is a microcosm of our world. As I turn the corner and start walking along the row of shops, I realize that this street is not such a bad reminder of the heavenly banquet that the Lord is planning for all of us: a feast of rich food and choice wines. I smile as I glance at the display of wine bottles in the window of the Lisbon Liquor Store—plenty there for lots of festive meals.

Reflection

Meditate on the passage cited in the scripture section that follows. Picture yourself seated at the messianic banquet in the kingdom. Who are the special people you're sure will be there with you? How does it feel to be with them?

Now, think of some people who you might be surprised or even disappointed to see there. Ask the Lord of the banquet, during these holy days, to help you to love as God loves, without boundaries or limits.

Sacred Scripture

On this mountain the Lord of hosts will make for all peoples, a feast of rich food, a feast of well-matured wines, of rich food filled with marrow, of well-matured wines strained clear. And he will destroy on this mountain the shroud that is cast over all peoples, the sheet that is spread over all nations; he will swallow up death forever. Then the Lord God will wipe away the tears from all faces, and the disgrace of his people he will take away from all the earth, for the Lord has spoken. (Isa. 25:6–8)

Rule of Benedict

To their fellow monks they show the pure love of brothers; to God, loving fear; to their abbot, unfeigned and humble love. Let them prefer nothing whatever to Christ, and may he bring us all together to everlasting life. (Chapter 72, "The Good Zeal of Monks," vv. 8–12)

DECEMBER 28

The Letdown

I glance up at the gray sky, wondering if it's going to snow. Then I tug my scarf a little tighter to keep out the dampness and, facing into the cold breeze, I continue, hands in my pockets, along the slate sidewalk. I've walked several blocks north from the monastery along King Boulevard, past the college campuses and Saint Michael's Hospital, and have turned down James Street. Passing the historic brick row houses, I notice a three-foot pine tree in a clay pot next to some brownstone steps, a few shiny ornaments clinging forlornly to its scrawny branches. As I reach University Avenue, everything is completely hushed, as if downtown were lying exhausted from the weeks of nonstop holiday shopping and celebrating. I decide to turn around and retrace my steps—I really don't feel like walking this morning.

My mood reflects the dull gray of the day itself. After the rich Christmas ceremonies in the monastery, the faculty parties, and the warm visits with family and friends, I'm feeling the familiar letdown, the post-Christmas blues. Returning alongside the back parking lot of Saint Michael's Hospital now, I remember that psychologists always report an increase in the number of cases of depression at this time of year. I don't think that it's due just to the cold and the long hours of darkness; it's because, for many of us, the holidays never deliver on their promises. They never live up to the romanticized images of Christmas that we see on television and in magazines: smiling, carefree families sitting around the fireplace, or horses pulling a wagon through the snow along a peaceful country road as their bells jangle merrily. Our own experience is always, by definition, much more mundane; it includes the stress of visiting difficult relatives, the weariness caused by all the running around and preparing for the celebration, even the weight we've gained from eating too much. In fact, by its very nature Christmas is destined to disappoint us: After all the hype from the prophets during Advent about the coming Prince of Peace and the ideal messianic age, all we get is a baby lying on straw in a manger.

I start to think how disappointed most people in the gospels were with Jesus himself. Jews who were looking for a military Messiah were frustrated when Jesus refused to lead a revolt to deliver them from the Romans. His followers were brokenhearted after his disgraceful death; as the two disciples on the way to Emmaus that first Easter morning said, "Our chief priests and leaders handed him over to be condemned to death and crucified him. But we had hoped that he was the one to redeem Israel" (Luke 24:20–21).

Then, as the risen Jesus began appearing to disciples, it became clear that the whole Christian life was going to depend on faith and on what could be seen with the eyes of faith alone. The early church began remembering Jesus teaching his disciples how to look at a grain of wheat and see in it a field of ripe wheat, or how to look at a mustard seed and see in it a tree filled with birds' nests. When Paul writes to the Corinthians, "We walk by faith and not by sight" (2 Cor. 5:7), he is referring to Jesus' earthly life from his appearance as a babe in Bethlehem to the enigma of the empty tomb, but he is also referring to our own lives as well, the joyful and the tragic parts, the sinful and the holy. The really important dimension of our lives can never be seen with simply human eyes. "My kingdom," Jesus tells Pilate, "does not belong to this world" (John 18:36).

As I walk up the last few yards of James Street toward King Boulevard, I realize that, like most Christians, I am accustomed—maybe too accustomed—to looking at the Christmas story with the eyes of faith. For example, I easily overlook the psychopathic murderer, Herod, who forces the holy family to flee hundreds of miles to Egypt to save the divine Child's life; I gloss over the horror of that same king's slaughtering of dozens of innocent babies. I easily see these incidents as part of the overall story of God's coming to earth to save us. Maybe part of the reason for my blue mood, then, is that I am forgetting to look at my own life the same way. Suppose I were to look again at the experiences of the past week with the eyes of faith? I would surely find, in the long and lovely liturgies, and in the presents from family and friends, a reflection of God's deep love for me. But I would also be able to look at the disappointments, the tiredness, the sense of sadness, and see in them, too, opportunities to grow closer to the newborn Christ. The letdown is a perfect opportunity to pray, asking the Lord who came and dwelt among us on Christmas morning to come and dwell with me today, and be a source of gladness when I'm sad, a source of strength when I'm weak, a source of hope when I'm doubtful.

I'm back at the corner of King Boulevard now and turn left to walk alongside the hospital again, where hundreds of people have bigger challenges than I in seeing their lives with the eyes of faith.

But at least the sun is starting to break through and brighten the sky.

Reflection

Look at your own experiences of the Christmas holidays—many of them enjoyable but others less so—and try to see how God was present to you in various people, events, and places. Then think of certain events in the past in which the Lord was present in a special way.

Sacred Scripture

So we are always confident; even though we know that while we are at home in the body we are away from the Lord—for we walk by faith, not by sight. (2 Cor. 5:6–7)

Wisdom of the Desert

Someone inquired of Father Abbot Nisteros the great, the friend of Abbot Anthony, asking: What good work shall I do? and that he replied: Not all works are alike. For scripture says that Abraham was hospitable and God was with him. Elias loved solitary prayer, and God was with him. And David was humble, and God was with him. Therefore, whatever you see your soul to desire according to God, do that thing, and you shall keep your heart safe.[27]

---

27. Thomas Merton, The Wisdom of the Desert (New York: New Directions, 1970), 25–26.

December 29
Bells

I'm on my way up the hill toward the monastery as the December sun sinks low behind some orange clouds in a pale blue sky. Suddenly I hear the bells ring out from the tower of the abbey church. Their call echoes off of the court house and the jail behind it, off of the Essex County College buildings and down Market Street, above the rumble of cars and the roar of busses, inviting everyone to five o'clock mass.

Listening to the joyful yet solemn sound of the bells, I start to think that it's no wonder that most cultures have given bells such an important place in religious and civil life. Great deep-voiced bells evoke a sense of the mysterious and mystical. Tiny bells lift the heart with feelings of delight and well-being. It's not surprising, either, that bells have become such a familiar part of our Christmas holidays: church bells ring out on Christmas morning, carillons play carols, while sleigh bells, silver bells, and jingle bells fill our holiday songs.

Following an ancient custom, each of our abbey bells has been given a saint's name. I listen closely, trying to pick out each one's distinct voice: there's the high tenor of the smallest one, Saint George, then the baritone of Saint Boniface, and the rich bass of Saint Liborius. The voice a little deeper than Saint George belongs to the fourth bell, whose name I don't know. The four have been singing together every day for over 130 years, blending their songs into a beautiful sound of praise.

As a Benedictine, I have a particular fondness for the sound of bells. In the early Middle Ages, when European culture and Roman civilization were disappearing under the onslaught of barbarian hordes, the monasteries became the centers of learning, of the arts and sciences—practically the only beacons of hope on a dark horizon. And so a monastery's bell, besides calling the monks to prayer, took on the important symbolic role of reminding everyone else in the neighborhood that God was still present even during the worst of times and that civilization and hope still survived in the presence of the monastery.

If the European monasteries were to properly fulfill their role of encouraging the people of the surrounding area, the sound of their bells would need to carry over longer distances, thus requiring bells of much better quality and resonance. So monks took up the craft of bell-making; they wrote the earliest treatises on the problems of harmonics and described their experiments with casting bells. The rich, solemn, joyful sound of today's church bells is the monks' legacy to us.

Listening to the call of Newark Abbey's bells echoing off of the buildings downtown, I wonder what the sound means to the hundreds of people who hear them: secondary school and college students, businessmen and commuters, teenage gang members, Muslim storekeepers, and our neighbors in the town houses? Whatever the different messages that individual people may get from them, the bells remind us monks of our responsibility to make our monastery what the bells proclaim it to be: a place of peace in the midst of busyness, of quiet in the midst of noise, of light in the midst of the shadows of poverty and addiction, of love in the midst of selfishness, violence, and racial tension.

Still walking up Branford Place and alongside our school's ball fields, I squint up at the tower high on the hill as the pealing of the bells begins to slow, and I realize once again just how pleasant they sound together. They fall silent just as I turn up King Boulevard toward the monastery.

It occurs to me that bells are beautiful heralds for the Christmas season, powerful reminders, as they were in the early Middle Ages, that the Christmas message is true: God has indeed become flesh and is still God-with-us right here in Newark, just as he was in first-century Palestine and eighth-century Europe.

Every day, in Newark Abbey's bell tower, Saint George, Saint Boniface, Saint Liborius, and their nameless friend continue a sacred tradition of reassuring a dark and frightened city that God is still present, still faithful, still loving us. Their job is, I suppose, the same as every Christian's: to carry the good news of God's presence wherever we go, whether by words or by actions. Each of us, just like those bells, can give people reason to hope in God's goodness.

I hurry up the front steps and into the monastery just in time for five o'clock mass.

Reflection

Bells are signs of God's constant loving presence in the everyday life of the world. Reflect on the kind of sign that you are to other people by your actions. What aspects of your life are most likely to be signs of hope and encouragement to those around you? Do your words, for example, carry a message of joy and hope, especially during this holy season, to people who may be sad and discouraged?

Sacred Scripture

You are the light of the world. A city built on a hill cannot be hid. No one after lighting a lamp puts it under the bushel basket, but on the lampstand, and it gives light to all in the house. In the same way, let your light shine before others, so that they may see your good works and give glory to your Father in heaven. (Matt. 5:14–16)

Rule of Benedict

Do not aspire to be called holy before you really are, but first be holy that you may more truly be called so. (Chapter 4, "The Tools for Good Works," v. 62)

DECEMBER 30
Returning Gifts

There are two people ahead of me in line at the cashier's counter in the big clothing store, which seems to be doing a steady business even though Christmas has been over now for a few days.

I feel a little guilty about what I'm about to do: my sister gave me a nice scarf for Christmas, but since I don't need another scarf, I'm returning it to the store to exchange it. What I need is the three pairs of socks that I'm holding.

As I wait my turn on line, I think about the thousands of people returning gifts they don't want—things that are the wrong size, the wrong color, or simply of no use. Even though my sister was thoughtful enough to include the gift receipt with her present in case I wanted to exchange it, I still feel uncomfortable.

As I check the price tags on my new socks and peer into the bag that holds the scarf from my sister, I start to think about how I deal with all the gifts I receive from God. It must give the Lord a lot of pleasure to see me accept those gifts with gratitude and humility and use them the way they were meant to be used—for helping other people, for giving God glory, for making others smile, for helping me to grow in love or wisdom.

It occurs to me that at times I treat some of God's gifts the way I'm treating my sister's. When I face a serious challenge, for example, which is a great opportunity for me to grow in trust by taking a risk, I say to God, "I don't really want this gift; may I please exchange it for one that is a little less frightening?" When I have a chance to grow in generosity and kindness by going out of my way for someone, I might say, "Well, there are lots of other ways to grow in virtue; I'll take one of them instead of this one." When the Lord offers me a perfect opportunity during a quiet prayer period to lay myself open to the divine will, I suddenly decide that I would rather be somewhere else doing something that's easier.

I'm next in line. I notice that the young woman in front of me is paying for a sweater with a gift certificate. I smile at the thought that God does not give gift certificates. We don't get to choose the exact gifts that we want, nor do we get to exchange them for something we think more suitable; instead we have to make do with the ones the Lord chooses for us.

"Next, please!"

The cashier's voice brings me back. I step up to the counter asking apologetically, "Could I please exchange this scarf for these socks?"

I take a furtive glance over my left shoulder, half afraid that my sister might come walking in.

"No problem!" answers the young woman behind the counter.

I hand over the scarf; she shoots its sales tag with a red ray from her barcode reader, and the deed is done. The scarf is no longer mine. Then she turns to the socks and does the same. After a couple of seconds the register starts to hum with a businesslike buzz and produces my new receipt.

"Have a happy day, sir!" says the cashier, handing me my socks in a bag. I accept it and smile.

"Thanks. Same to you."

With my new gifts in hand, I turn and head for the exit. On the way past the racks of pants and the shelves of sweaters, I start to wonder how many gifts from God I have refused recently. I think of an opportunity I had last week to change my own agenda to make a phone call to a friend who needed to hear from me, but I didn't bother. Guess I missed that gift. I'm sure there were a few others in the past few weeks, such as the chance to help a student who was hoping for a little attention from me, but I was too tired or too busy.

I step briskly through the magnetic detectors and out of the store, grateful for the new socks from my sister, and wondering what gifts the Lord still has in store for me.

Reflection

Think of a recent "gift" that you received from the Lord, which, while unwelcome at the time, turned out to be a source of growth for you in some way. Perhaps it was an event that forced you out of your comfortable habits, or some challenge to let go of a certain way of thinking. Can you think of a "gift" which you have been given by God, but which you have not really accepted or used?

Sacred Scripture

For by grace you have been saved through faith, and this is not your own doing; it is the gift of God—not the result of works, so that no one may boast. For we are what he has made us, created in Christ Jesus for good works, which God prepared beforehand to be our way of life. (Eph. 2:8–10)

Rule of Benedict

If anyone is offered something by a superior and refuses it, then, if later he wants what he refuses or anything else, he should receive nothing at all until he has made appropriate amends. (Chapter 43, "Tardiness at the Work of God or at Table," v. 19)

DECEMBER 31
New Year's Eve

The abbey church is quiet at ten o'clock on this last night of the year. I'm spending the final hours keeping vigil with a few other people, preparing to welcome the new year at midnight. At 11:15 there will be a prayer service followed by mass, but for now I sit in the semidarkness and enjoy the silence. Twelve little candles flicker along the walls, and large poinsettia plants glow burgundy around the base of the statute of the black Virgin of Monserrat up near the monks' choir stalls.

Each New Year's Eve since the new millennium, the abbey has sponsored this all-night vigil, using the last night of the year as a time for reflection and prayer. I pick up my prayer journal and start to look back through its pages, reflecting on the past year. As I wait here in the serene stillness, my mind suddenly wanders to a very different scene less than twenty miles away, in Manhattan.

Right now about a million people are crowding into Times Square amid dazzling lights and bustling energy, at the symbolic center of New York City. In a couple of hours they, along with an estimated one billion people watching on television, will cheer as the famous sparkling New Year's Eve ball descends from the flagpole atop One Times Square. There will be fireworks, balloons, and tons of confetti to bid farewell to the past year and welcome in the new one.

I continue looking through the journal pages I've written over the past twelve months, rereading little pieces of my own salvation history.

Parishioners are starting to arrive for the 11:15 service. A young couple in bright, colorful African dress slip into the back row with a little boy already fast asleep in his father's arms.

New Year's Eve is the time when the two contrasting themes of the Advent and Christmas seasons come together. The first theme is the Advent one of waiting for the kingdom to come. It is not yet here, but we are waiting for it to be inaugurated when Christ returns one day in glory at the end of time to bring us and all creation to fulfillment. In fact, the human experience that the kingdom is not yet here is at the root of a New Year's custom: superstitious people would make all sorts of loud noises on New Year's Eve, banging pots together or shooting off fireworks in hopes of driving demons away as the new year was about to begin. Maybe this is why we salute the new year with noisemakers and fireworks—and the pealing of church bells.

But the bells also bring to mind a second theme, the joyful news of Christmas, that salvation is now present among us in the form of a newborn babe. The Letter to the Hebrews begins with the words, "In many and various ways God spoke of old to our fathers by the prophets; but in these last days he has spoken to us by a Son" (Heb. 1:1–2). The kingdom is already here, because Emmanuel, God-with-us, has already conquered death and sin. We ring the bells to celebrate the arrival of the kingdom.

But midnight is still two hours away. I turn back to my journal and start to notice how my own life seems to fluctuate between the two themes of the "already" and the "not yet." There are reflections from months ago asking the Lord to help me and give me strength in the face of some trial, there is a lament over a young man murdered in the street a couple of blocks from here, and there's an act of contrition. These are prayers from the "not-yet," asking the Lord to bring the kingdom to completion soon. Then there are just as many entries, some of them only a sentence or two, that celebrate God's overwhelming goodness to me, thanking the Lord for bringing me through a difficult ordeal, or for being so obviously present at one of our community meetings. These are prayers from the "already," reveling in the saving presence of the Lord.

In a little while, at the stroke of midnight, as we start to sing the Gloria of the mass, the tower bells will peal out in celebration of the new year. But, come to think of it, I wouldn't mind if their sound scared away, for a year or so, the demons of crime and despair, of drugs and gang violence, of racism and injustice that keep the kingdom from arriving in Newark.

I take out my ballpoint pen and start writing my thanks for the year that is ending and my hopes for the new one that is about to begin.

Reflection

Think of some happy events during the past year that let you experience God's loving kindness. Then think of some events which show that the reign of God is still incomplete (for example sickness, sin, and suffering). Did you experience God's presence during these times as well?

Sacred Scripture

Pray then in this way: Our Father in heaven, hallowed be your name. Your kingdom come. (Matt. 6:9–10)

Rule of Benedict

Yearn for everlasting life with holy desire. Day by day remind yourself you are going to die. (Chapter 4, "Instruments for Good Works," vv. 46–47)

JANUARY 1

New Beginnings

I'm walking back up Market Street from Penn Station on my first walk of the year. The first of January always gives me a sense of a new beginning. I have a nice new calendar for my office with beautiful color photos of European cities to remind me that I'm setting out on a brand new year.

As I continue up Market Street in the bright sunshine admiring the new Prudential Center sports arena off to my left, a middle-aged woman strides toward me, heading, I presume, for the train station. Her long, dark green coat looks brand new. I glance down at my new gloves—a Christmas present. I start thinking about how much I enjoy new things: a brand new book, a new school term with a classroom full of new faces, a new calendar, and even my new gloves.

Then I think back to the half-hour I spent after lunch with my Bible. I sat down with my Greek New Testament and a Greek lexicon to study once again the two biblical words meaning "new." I do this at the start of each new year. First there is the familiar word for "new," *neos*, which describes a new version of something else, such as the new wine in the old wineskins, and the new covenant established in place of the old one. This is the kind of newness I like: refreshing, upbeat, and pleasant.

But, unfortunately, there is a second word for "new," *kainos*, which reflects a very different kind of newness. It refers to something previously unheard of and unthought of, something entirely different from anything that went before. I find this sort of newness very unsettling. As a creature of habit I enjoy the predictability of the familiar and am wary of the totally unknown; I try to avoid such radical newness whenever possible. Unfortunately, though, it is precisely this unsettling kind of new, *kainos*, that shows up in the most crucial passages of the New Testament. After years of rereading them I can list them from memory.

There is the passage in Ephesians: "Put on the new self, created in God's way in righteousness and holiness of truth" (Eph. 4:24). When Paul writes this, he is not talking about some cosmetic "makeover" of my old self in which I remain essentially unchanged inside; the self he is calling me to be is an entirely new person, not just *neos* but *kainos*.

Then in the Second Letter to the Corinthians we read about this radical newness again: "So whoever is in Christ is a new [*kainos*] creation: the old things have passed away; behold new [*kainos*] things have come" (2 Cor. 5:17 NAB).

A noun form of *kainos* comes up in the sixth chapter of Romans: "just as Christ was raised from the dead by the glory of the Father, we too might live in newness [*kainotēs*] of life" (Rom. 6:4 NAB). This is not a pleasant gradual renewal of my life as I presently know it; rather it is an uprooting of the familiar, a totally unforeseen and undreamed-of existence.

As I cross Mulberry Street and start along a block of rundown stores, arcades, and eateries, I think to myself that we could certainly use some urban renewal around here. This reminds me that while I may enjoy all the "new" things that the coming year promises, the unsettling truth is that being *neos*, "new and improved," is simply not good enough; this is not what I am called to be as a Christian.

Nowhere in the gospels does Jesus ever call me to gradually improve and become renewed [*neos*]; he does call me, however, to risk letting go of everything that I am, everything that I have accomplished, everything that I am familiar with, in order to become *kainos*, a new person whom I cannot even foresee or imagine—the person God has in mind. Saint Paul says it this way: "I have been crucified with Christ; yet I live, no longer I, but Christ lives in me" (Gal. 2:19–20 NAB). The coming of Christ at Christmas is meant to transform me into a new person, not just someone *neos*, merely an improved version of the old me.

As I approach the busy intersection of Broad and Market, I can see the new lampposts and the new planters and road dividers along Broad Street. Walking past the last of the rundown stores on Market Street, I start to wonder what this new year might be like for me if I were to let God transform me into someone new. I begin to ask the Lord to help me to be open to the challenges that will come during this new year, especially those that will call me to become someone truly *kainos*, a new being completely beyond even my best dreams.

Reflection

"So whoever is in Christ is a new [*kainos*] creation: the old things have passed away; behold new [*kainos*] things have come" (2 Cor. 5:17). Can you think of something "old," comfortable, and familiar that the Lord may be asking you to let go of during these holy days in order to make you into an entirely new creation? Will you resist the change? Welcome it? Accept it grudgingly?

Sacred Scripture

Then I saw a new [*kainos*] heaven and a new [*kainos*] earth; for the first heaven and the first earth had passed away, and the sea was no more. And I saw the holy city, the new [*kainos*] Jerusalem, coming down out of heaven from God, prepared as a bride adorned for her husband. And I heard a loud voice from the throne saying, "See, the home of God is among mortals. He will dwell with them; they will be his peoples, and God himself will be with them." (Rev. 21:1–3)

Rule of Benedict

Do not be daunted immediately by fear and run away from the road that leads to salvation. It is bound to be narrow at the outset. But as we progress in this way of life and in faith, we shall run on the path of God's commandments, our hearts overflowing with the inexpressible delight of love. (Prologue, vv. 48–49)

Epilogue

I hope that our walks together around the city have helped you to experience the holidays as truly holy days. As the holiday season draws to a close with the coming of the new year, this book could, of course, come to a close as well. But these meditative looks at reality do not have to end. In fact, my hope is that you will continue to see the world with a contemplative eye all year round, taking long, loving looks at the familiar people and simple events around you. As you move through the streets of your town, and indeed through the journey of your life, may you discover there the faithful, loving God who keeps being born into our world all the time, and whose unseen presence turns every day into a holy day.